HELVETIA

Dedication

To my grandfather, Herman Schneider, whose dream as a young Sankt Gallen schoolboy was to be a farmer, and whose dream came true in America.

With special appreciation to my parents, Edward and Helen Sutton.

And to Eleanor Fahrner Mailloux for holding it all together for all these years!

Helvetia

THE HISTORY OF A SWISS VILLAGE
IN THE MOUNTAINS OF WEST VIRGINIA

By David H. Sutton

West Virginia University Press

MORGANTOWN 2010

WVU Press gratefully acknowledges the financial assistance provided for this book by the Helvetia Restoration and Development Organization.

West Virginia University Press, Morgantown 26505

Copyright 2010 West Virginia University Press

All rights reserved.

First edition published in 1990 by Peter Lang Publishing, Inc.

Second edition 2010.

ISBN-10: 1-933202-56-4

ISBN-13: 978-1-933202-56-3

(alk. paper)

Library of Congress Cataloguing in Publication Data

Sutton, David H.

Helvetia : the history of a Swiss village in the mountains of West Virginia / by David H. Sutton. -- 2nd ed.

p.   cm.

First edition published in 1990 by Peter Lang Publishing, under title One's own hearth is like gold : a history of Helvetia, West Virginia.

Includes bibliographical references and index.

ISBN-13: 978-1-933202-56-3 (pbk. : alk. paper)

ISBN-10: 1-933202-56-4 (pbk. : alk. paper)

1. Swiss Americans--West Virginia--Helvetia--History. 2. Immigrants--West Virginia--Helvetia--History. 3. Helvetia (W. Va.)--History. 4. Helvetia (W. Va.)--Social life and customs. 5. Community life--West Virginia--Helvetia--History. 6. Social change--West Virginia--Helvetia--History. 7. Farm life--West Virginia--Helvetia--History. 8. Mountain life--West Virginia--Helvetia--History. I. Sutton, David H. One's own hearth is like gold. II. Title.

F249.H45S88 2010

975.4'85--dc22

Library of Congress Control Number: 2009047239

Book design by Than Saffel. Layout by Michael Rabjohns. Edited by Danielle Zahoran.

Table of Contents

Table of Contents (cont'd)

Acknowledgments

THE PUBLICATION of a community's history is always a special occasion, and it inevitably brings to mind all the special people who contributed. There are far too many to mention in a few paragraphs, but every contribution has been greatly appreciated.

The greatest debt is owed to the people of Helvetia themselves, who opened their doors and attics and willingly subjected themselves to hours of tape-recorded interviews in the name of history. They are still family after all these years.

Several research and funding institutions were also involved. I received invaluable assistance from the staff at the West Virginia and Regional History Collection, archivists Gerald Arlettaz at the Swiss National Archives, Hirschi Ernst at the Cantonal Archive of Bern, and Dr. Jean Jacques Siegrist at the Cantonal Archive of Aargau. The Humanities Foundation of West Virginia provided grant support for a community oral history project, and the West Virginia Department of Culture and History gave a technical assistance grant for photo reproduction and preservation.

Countless individuals have also given of their time and energy throughout the research and writing. In Switzerland, these include Alwin and Anni Schneider, Kurt Welte, and Agathon Aerni. In the United States, special contributions were made by Marc King, Paul Daniels, Lorraine Duisit, Eleanor Mailloux, Don Teter, Judy Bard, Ken Sullivan, Leo Schelbert, Erdmann Schmocker, Chau Nguyen, Sally McDaniel, Rogers McAvoy, Chip Hicks, members of the Helvetia Historical Society, and many others.

In this second edition, I received tremendous help with photographic materials from Eleanor Betler, Woody Higginbotham, Dave Whipp, Bruce Cressler, Steve Shaluta, and Norton Gusky. In manuscripts, Dan Lehmann and Curator John Cuthbert at the West Virginia and Regional History Collection were there when I needed them most.

The staff at West Virginia University Press have been so able, willing, and professionally adept at what they do that working on the project with them has been a tremendous pleasure. Thank you all!

Author's Note

THIS IS THE SECOND EDITION of a book first published in 1990 by Peter Lang Publishers entitled *One's Own Hearth Is Like Gold: A History of Helvetia, West Virginia*. Only 1000 copies were printed and quickly sold, leaving the book out of print for many years.

In 2009, West Virginia University Press offered to create a second and updated edition. I was happy for the opportunity to get the book back in print and to add additional text and photographs from more recent times.

The main body of the work remains the same, but I have written a new introduction giving a brief but sweeping account of the major themes of Helvetia events during the past fifty years. I was also delighted to have access to a wealth of more recent photographic material, which we have fashioned into a wonderful photographic essay. All this adds to the rich and ongoing tapestry that is Helvetia. I hope you enjoy the result.

David H. Sutton
September 2009

Introduction to the Second Edition

ON A WARM summer morning in Helvetia, you will likely be greeted by birdsong, the gentle rippling of flowing water, the smell of clear mountain air and freshly cut grass. If you venture out in the early hours, you may see young fawns in the meadow, a plump groundhog munching the dew-covered grass, or a silent hawk circling for a morning hunt. Helvetia is not completely isolated from the outside world—there is some traffic on the small mountain road, and you may even encounter a noisy log truck with its screeching brakes. But as the clamor fades into the distance, it is easy to drop back into the natural beauty of Helvetia's mountain setting.

As the sun begins to peek over the hilltop, giving everything in the valley a golden tone, you will already find Heidi Arnett busy with the morning mail in the post office and store. Heidi is a fourth-gener-ation Swiss descendent of the Fahrner family from Canton Zürich. Most mornings Heidi is too busy to chat about family history, but a hot cup of coffee awaits you at the Hütte Restaurant, where owner Eleanor Fahrner Mailloux (Heidi's mother) will fill your tummy with muesli and tales of old Helvetia.

After a relaxing breakfast, a half-mile walk to the community cemetery provides great exercise and a chance to appreciate the many German-language gravestones marking the lives of the local Swiss and German settlers. The way back brings you by the Cheese Haus, and Beekeeper Inn, the town's bed and breakfast. A shortcut through the grass behind the inn will bring you to the historic square containing the settlers' cabin museum, town library, one-room school and gazebo. Just above, the ever-present church keeps watch, signaling the passage of time with its chimes. You stand now at the center of the village, on the same ground cleared and tilled by five generations of Swiss settlers and their descendants. The history of the village is palpable, yet this is not the same Helvetia of settlement years, of thriving agricultural years, or even post-World War II change. The Helvetia you witness today began to take shape in the 1960s.

During this time, the entire village was placed on the National Register of Historic Places. The Hütte Restaurant was started, with its tasty Swiss German recipes, together with an adjacent gift shop for tourists. Swiss folk dancing, which had been part of an earlier revival, was reestablished to teach young people the traditional dances and to perform for audiences. The Germanic pre-Lenten festival of *Fastnacht*, not widely practiced in this mostly Protestant community, found rich soil to grow in the fun-loving atmosphere. As this new energy spread, it also reinvigorated older events like the Community Fair, Fourth of July Celebration, and annual Ramp Dinner. The Swiss National Holiday was also added to the community calendar. Helvetia experienced the beginning of a small, intimate tourist trade that infused the community with much-needed cash to help maintain its community-owned properties and expand the local economy.

This new era profited from the talents of an outside investor named Delores Baggerly. She visited the community in the mid-1960s as a friend of Eleanor Mailloux. Baggerly was intrigued by the possibilities of economic development in rural areas and came at a time when local real estate was available. She and her husband purchased three central properties in the village from which she created a restaurant and gift shop, what later became the Beekeeper Inn, and a public open space, "The Meadow," with an outdoor stage for programs and performances.

All of these were ordinary homes to which Baggerly added gingerbread trim, Swiss-style railings, bright colors, and window boxes filled with flowers. Mrs. Baggerly's activities helped to preserve Helvetia, but she was not a historic preservationist in the traditional sense. She was really an artist, painting on a real-world canvas a scene of her own Swiss village. Her influence has been lasting, but her stay was a short four years, as she became ill and left to seek treatment and rest.

The properties and businesses she began were purchased by Eleanor Mailloux in the early 1970s. Eleanor had served in the American Red Cross during World War II, and had lived and traveled extensively in the Far East before moving back to Helvetia in the mid-1960s to raise her family. Eleanor also had an artistic flair and a dogged determination to see the community with its Swiss roots continue and thrive. She maintained and expanded the restaurant and gift shop, started the Beekeeper Inn in 1983, and was active in the Restoration and Development Association, Alpine Rose Garden Club, and other community groups. On every issue relating to community development and historic preservation, from school consolidation, to better roads, to the threat of massive power lines, Eleanor has been a constant advocate. She has made Helvetia her cause, and her service to the community will be felt and remembered far into the future.

By the late 1970s, Helvetia was losing its remaining second- and third-generation Swiss Americans to old age. During this time, I began work on what became the first full history of the community. With a small grant from the West Virginia Humanities Foundation, I recorded over two dozen oral history interviews with older Helvetians who remembered the years between 1900 and 1980. Document research also brought to light letters and papers regarding the settlement years that had never been explored. These led to sources in Swiss archives that were rich in details about Helvetia and other Swiss settlements in West Virginia and surrounding states. All this would bear fruit for the story that follows and create a very full bibliography of Helvetia sources.

The oral history project also brought a treasure trove of photographs and negatives to my attention. While doing interviews, people would frequently rummage through their closets or albums and give me old photos for preservation. Some years before, Eleanor Mailloux had salvaged several hundred glass plate negatives taken by the Aegerter family between approximately 1890 and 1915. I carefully printed these negatives and showed them to older members of the community for identification. Many were still in excellent condition, and I selected some of the best images for a photo exhibition funded by the West Virginia Department of Culture and History. After showings in Charleston and Morgantown, the photos were hung in the community hall. The entire photo collection is preserved at the West Virginia and Regional History Collection at West Virginia University. Today, Eleanor Betler continues the process of collecting and cataloging Helvetia documents and photographs at the community archive.

The energy of the revival also brought greatly needed community services to Helvetia in the form of health care and information technologies. In 1976 a small health clinic was added to the village with a full-time doctor, Michael Rosenberg. His wife Jane was instrumental in starting the local library, now an important resource for both young and old Helvetians. After decades of wrangling over school consolidation in the county, in 2005 a new state-of-the-art K–12 school was built at Pickens to serve the local communities. And, in an unusually ambitious plan, the Adrian Public Service District provided public water service to Helvetia and Czar in the fall of 2009. As some local springs and wells had been adversely affected by underground mining operations in the area in the past two decades, this was a helpful project to many.

Another important economic project in recent years was the expansion of cheese-making facilities in the village. The community received a grant to equip a professional cheese operation housed in the old Cheese Haus. A large 265-gallon vat and other equipment came from The Netherlands and was in operation for about three years. However, the enlarged plant arrived as the last vestiges of small, family dairy farming were ending, and it has suffered from a lack of milk and a long-term cheesemaker. This will continue to be an important challenge going forward, both for the local economy and the long tradition of Swiss cheesemaking in the community.

Despite new business activity in Helvetia, the local economy has had many ups and downs in the past five decades. Apart from tourism and agriculture, small lumber and coal operations continued to supply a few jobs throughout the latter half of the century. Some of the narrow seams of coal in the area were sought after for their low sulfur content, and a coal-washing plant was built at nearby Star Bridge to clean the coal for market. Coal was also shipped on the Pickens B&O Line for many years, but even the railroad and coal processing at Pickens eventually gave way in the early 1990s. Operations at Star Bridge continued, but followed a very uneven path, as the price of coal fluctuated widely with the volatile oil market. Absent a local sawmill after the 1960s, timber that was cut was trucked to Mill Creek, Elkins, or Buckhannon to be processed. Helvetia continued, as it always had, to be on the fringes of the industrial economy.

The slow decline in the industrial economy was reflected in a continued loss of population. As the last half the twentieth century unfolded, Helvetia lost more and more farms, and more young people left for college and professions in surrounding towns and states. The size of families shrank, grandparents died,

and despite a few new residents, there was a net loss of people. Today residents number about fifty in the village, and an additional eighty in the surrounding area. The local school, which includes children from Pickens and Czar, has about forty students from kindergarten through high school.

Through all the changes that have occurred in the past fifty years, Helvetia remains a lively community inhabited by a few self-reliant people. Although public water and high-speed Internet have made their way to town, it is still an hour's drive to the nearest grocery store. There is no movie theater, no shopping mall, no Walmart. Cell phone signals do not penetrate the valley, and no one even cares where the nearest Starbucks might be!

Helvetia is a place apart from the mainstream culture, and most who live there see that as a good thing. It offers a simple, rugged way of life, built on the foundations of Swiss-European traditions that have stood the test of time. Perhaps what is needed most today are more community members to fill volunteer community jobs. As Eleanor Mailloux recently joked, "We need more immigrants!" It seems that after 140 years the town has come full circle.

If you are interested in this intriguing circle and how it has progressed from its beginning in 1869, please read and enjoy the following pages. And next time you're in town for the monthly square dance or a hearty meal, ask what you can do to help this very special place retain its unique traditions and way of life for future generations.

Preface

HELVETIA, WEST VIRGINIA, is a German Swiss settlement tucked away in the highlands of West Virginia since its beginning in 1869. It is one of many small, ethnic communities founded throughout the United States in the last century, which offered a sense of identity and a cultural buffer zone to their members. The community is part of a much larger movement of Europeans into the United States, and represents only a tiny segment of the Swiss migration. Yet, to fully understand it as a unique expression of these trends, it must be placed in a regional context. Only by focusing on Swiss migration into the central Appalachian region is it possible to understand the forces that shaped Helvetia's existence and that of other Swiss communities in West Virginia, Kentucky, and Tennessee.

The importance of this context becomes apparent when one examines where in the United States the Swiss tended to settle in the nineteenth century. Of the 200,000 Swiss who came to America between 1820 and 1900, a full 40 percent settled in cities. The majority (60 percent) most often chose rural places where there was excellent farmland and available markets. As one historian has aptly observed, "[The Swiss] preferred to settle in an area that had a maximum advantage for normal economic and social life."[1] Why, then, did a small segment of immigrants move to the most desolate sections of the Appalachians, where farmland was poor and where they were extremely isolated from economic centers? Further, what were the backgrounds and characteristics of this group? What types of communities did they form economically and culturally? To what extent did their isolation contribute to the retention of European cultural traditions? How was their experience similar to or different from other Swiss immigrants who arrived in America in the last century? These central questions are raised by a regional focus, and they form the major themes of the following chapters.

The history of Helvetia resembles the history of several other Swiss settlements in the region in terms of its isolated location, the lack of planning which surrounded its founding, the speculative nature of land sales, the type of person who moved there, and the local settlement patterns. Simply because of where they chose to live, these Swiss had much in common with one another. Their lives and experiences were quite different from their compatriots who farmed the fertile lands of the Midwest or who became merchants and bankers in America's large urban centers. The story of the Swiss in the Appalachians is more one of isolation and subsistence than of prosperity.

The Swiss settlements that were founded in West Virginia, Kentucky, and Tennessee at the end of the nineteenth century have not received a great deal of attention from researchers and writers. Guy Metraux, one of the first scholars to take note of the settlements wrote in his 1949 dissertation that the writings about Swiss in West Virginia did not correspond in "quality and information" to those available in Tennessee and Kentucky. He could have added, correctly, that research on the Swiss in all three

states was far behind that of other areas. The situation has changed little in the past forty years. Magazine and newspaper articles abound with quaint stories, but few have attempted to sift through the sources for an accurate or thoughtful history. There are two notable exceptions. In 1960, Dr. Elizabeth Cometti published an article on Swiss immigration to West Virginia, documenting the role of land speculators in the settlement of Swiss in West Virginia. The article is a cornerstone for understanding the communities of Helvetia, Adolph, and Alpena in Randolph County. Later, in 1965, graduate student Atje Partadiredja at the University of Wisconsin collected a large amount of data on Helvetia, which he assembled into a PhD dissertation. He did not, however, arrive at any meaningful synthesis of the material, leaving the task of interpretation essentially undone. These two pieces of writing are the only new contributions to our knowledge of Swiss settlements in the region in several decades. Such a gap underlines the most basic contribution of a history of Helvetia—that of providing an interpretative approach to one such settlement that can be compared to other Swiss American communities.

The reader will note that although the settlements have been cast as predominantly "Swiss" in makeup, they attracted primarily German Swiss— that is, Swiss from the German speaking areas of Switzerland, rather than those from the French or Italian areas. They were, therefore, not representative of all Swiss. Further, German immigrants were also attracted to the settlements. In the case of Helvetia, approximately 25 percent of the population was of German origin. Although distinctions can be made between these two groups, the southern Germans were very similar in culture and outlook to the German Swiss. In fact, the two groups had more in common than Swiss of different language groups. It seems appropriate then, to treat Helvetia as a German Swiss community with a significant group of German settlers who felt an affinity to the cultural and linguistic traditions that were present. The settlement of Germans and Swiss together in America deserves more attention that can be given it here.

Finally, the reader should be aware that this is an exercise in local history, written by a local writer. The task of writing the history of one's own community is an extremely difficult one. I have tried to avoid the usual pitfalls of the local historian, but without doubt, my long relationship with Helvetia has to some extent determined my approach and affected my choice of topics. The historian who wishes to write more than an encyclopedia of facts or a collection of genealogies is faced with constant choices in selecting the most important aspects of his or her topic. These are perhaps not the choices that would be made by others, now or in the future, but they are offered as a contribution to a larger understanding of Helvetia and the Swiss in America. It is hoped that the strengths of the study outweigh its inevitable weaknesses and that all who read it will gain some new insight into what it means to be an immigrant and a Helvetian.

Chapter 1

The Immigration of Swiss to America and Migrations to the Central Appalachian Mountains

BETWEEN 1821 AND 1924 an estimated fifty-five million Europeans left their homes for other lands. Of these, the Swiss were a tiny group of about 332,000. Although they scattered around the globe, most went to North America where the climate, resources, and economic opportunity seemed most favorable.[1] Their individual reasons for leaving were diverse, their choices of where to settle often based on inaccurate information about the new land. Yet, certain patterns in the scramble to board a ship sailing for America are discernible.

While the perception of opportunity in a specific region or city was a strong factor in where people settled, conditions at home most often caused people to uproot. In the nineteenth century, the reasons for emigration were predominantly economic. The periods of highest migration occurred when agrarian dislocation and unemployment caused by the Industrial Revolution, together with crop failures, made emigration a thinkable alternative. The year of 1816 in Europe was such a time. Record cold caused widespread crop failures all over the continent. In Switzerland, snow fell every month, ruining all the harvests; bread prices rose 800 percent. These events, combined with high unemployment in the cotton industry, caused many to leave Switzerland and other parts of Europe. Following this crisis, Swiss emigration slowed until the 1840s when mechanization of the weaving industry took many jobs. In 1843 and 1846–47, Swiss farmers again suffered heavy potato and grain failures, causing the number of emigrants during the following years to swell far beyond previous numbers. The wave peaked in 1854 with some 8,000 Swiss moving to the

United States. Most of these were farmers seeking good, cheap land who settled in the eastern Mississippi Valley.[2]

Due to the Panic of 1857 and the Civil War in the United States, the flow of Swiss was reduced to moderate numbers throughout the 1860s and 1870s. However, in the early 1880s, Swiss immigration increased dramatically as the American Midwest flooded Europe with cheap grain, causing a general collapse in Western European agriculture. In 1883, Swiss migration to the United States reached its peak, as some 12,500 new immigrants arrived in a one-year period. This trend, reinforced by an industrial depression in 1885–86, contributed to high emigration through the end of the decade. Swiss emigration never again reached these proportions. Those who came to the U.S. settled predominantly in the regions of Indiana, Illinois, Wisconsin, and Michigan, where farmland was excellent and developing towns and rail centers provided growing markets. After 1890 emigration steadily declined. Relatively small numbers of Swiss farmers settled in Washington, Oregon, and California. Others went to urban centers, particularly New York City, as the cause of emigration became less agricultural in nature and more due to the attraction of business and scientific opportunities in the United States. A more stable Swiss economy also made staying at home a favorable option once again.[3]

The vast majority of Swiss who arrived in these migrations to America were not the undesirable elements of society, as is sometimes charged. They were most often dislocated farmers or lower middle-class artisans and semi-skilled workers who did not want to give up their agrarian or trade pursuits for wage labor in factories. Most had at least the basic means to start a new life, and some received considerable help from their local communities in Switzerland.[4] American consuls in Switzerland, however, accused the Swiss of sending large numbers of paupers to the United States. They pointed to the fact that some Swiss communities used forced emigration as a way to clear their welfare rolls of paupers whom they would normally have to support. Since every citizen owned a share of community grazing and forest land, a person was sometimes given the calculated cash value of his portion and sent across the ocean. This practice was labeled *Seelenverkauferei*, or the sale of souls, by opponents and led to some vigorous diplomatic activity between the United States and Switzerland in the 1850s and again in the 1880s. Although such overt practices of forced emigration appalled American consuls, there is no reason to believe that Switzerland sent any greater percentage of poor to the States than did other European countries. In fact, the overwhelming praise of Swiss immigrants as ambitious, energetic, industrious, and honest, from every front, including from the consuls themselves, suggests that the majority were actually desirable candidates for American citizenship.[5]

Swiss emigration, then, must be understood in the context of the Industrial Revolution. The economic conditions in Switzerland, and to some extent those in the United States, shaped the ebb and flow of Swiss migration in the nineteenth century. However, to stop there would be to ignore some lesser but important factors in the case of the Swiss, nor would it help us explain the rather consistent flow of people in times of relative economic ease.

Various authors have suggested that the Swiss have a certain predisposition for traveling, a wanderlust, which helped propel them aboard. Certainly some immigrants' writing expresses this. The early heritage of the Swiss mercenaries also set a precedent in Switzerland and in Europe for emigration based solely on profit. Yet, if these traditions and the wanderlust did play a role in nineteenth-century Swiss culture, it surfaced in only a small percentage of the population. Ultimately, most Swiss opted to stay at home and live as best they could. [6]

A much more important factor was the type and accuracy of the information the prospective emigrants received about conditions in a new land. The number of positive reports from relatives, while difficult to gauge, came as a trusted source of information which encouraged many and helped foster a "favorable climate of opinion" about emigration.[7] Such letters were also related to the more calculated propaganda of American railroads, land agents, and colonizers, who had a vested interest in maintaining the tides of immigration. These types of information often gave a skewed testimony of the new life. The Swiss and others, particularly those who did not speak English, were often misled by the contrivings of people who used them to their own advantage. In the case of various Swiss settlements in the Americas, and especially for Swiss migration to the Appalachians, the role of misleading information was a significant factor in shaping where immigrants located and how they reacted to their new environment.[8]

American colonizers also had their counterparts in Europe, as emigration societies, agents, railroads, and ship lines all benefited from the great movement of people. The port of Le Havre developed a virtual monopoly on Swiss emigrant travel by offering reduced train fares and running special trains in the spring season. Individual agents in Switzerland and elsewhere who represented special interests in the United States sometimes resorted to misleading tactics in order to send people to a certain location. In some cases, these representatives promised land to prospective emigrants sight-unseen and shipped them off to discover too late that the property was undesirable.[9]

Although it is a popular idea that Swiss emigrants were naturally attracted to mountainous areas abroad because of their familiarity with mountain regions in Switzerland, there is little to support this assertion. Most Swiss either chose to dwell in urban areas, such as New York City, or in farming communities outside North America's mountain regions. Good agricultural land was a prime concern, and those states which offered gently rolling and flat land were most often chosen as their new homes. Until the

1880s, Ohio was the chief recipient of Swiss settlers in the nation. Following Ohio, by the number of Swiss inhabitants, were Illinois, New York, Missouri, Wisconsin, Pennsylvania, Indiana, and Iowa. All provided not only good farmland, but easy access from ports of entry and established lines of communication such as rail and postal services.[10] "The Swiss," wrote one historian, "except in isolated and exceptional circumstances, was not a pioneer. He hesitated before going into the wilderness to open the land."[11] Although sometimes an experienced farmer in Europe, the immigrant was generally unfamiliar with American soils and other conditions. He had little training or experience for farming in rugged, unsettled territory, and only in a few instances did he attempt it.

The exceptions to this rule occurred in the central Appalachians. Despite warnings from several sectors, both in the United States and Switzerland, about the risks and hardships involved in settling in this region, a few Swiss did exactly that. By the end of the largest emigration period in 1890, at least 3,529 Swiss were living in approximately fifteen towns and settlements scattered through the mountains of Tennessee, Kentucky, and West Virginia.[12] The history of each settlement differs in detail, but a common thread connects them. The ways in which they were founded, the type of person attracted, and the patterns of settlement, are quite similar.

Of the three states considered here, Kentucky contained the largest number of Swiss by 1890. In addition to a sizeable Swiss population living in Louisville, the Kentucky Bureau of Geology and Immigration carefully fostered the settlement of Bernstadt in Laurel County. Bernstadt, named for the capital of the Swiss Confederation, was founded in 1881 by wealthy Swiss inventor Karl Imobersteg and his consultant, Otto Brunner, an agricultural teacher from the canton of Zürich. Imobersteg supplied the funds to purchase 40,000 acres of land in rugged eastern Kentucky, some eighty miles south of Lexington. Brunner was to be the land agent and agricultural specialist for the community. He was joined on the site by Paul Schenk, the son of a prominent Swiss president, who moved to Kentucky after a short stay in West Virginia. Schenk's presence gave both notoriety among Swiss and a certain legitimacy to the endeavor, and the two men teamed up to divide and sell the land in small parcels. They publicized the settlement both in the United States and Switzerland. Brunner went so far as to visit people in Switzerland to persuade them to move to Kentucky. In 1881, forty-two families (most from the canton of Bern) moved onto the Bernstadt land. The colony grew quickly, reaching a population of 465 by 1886. Brunner, however, was accused of swindling the settlers of their land payments, and after an investigation, he "disappeared between dark and sunrise." Paul Schenk stayed and continued to advertise the progress of the settlement, but immigration slowed greatly when Brunner's actions became known abroad.[13]

Swiss settlements in the Central Appalachians, 1860–1890.

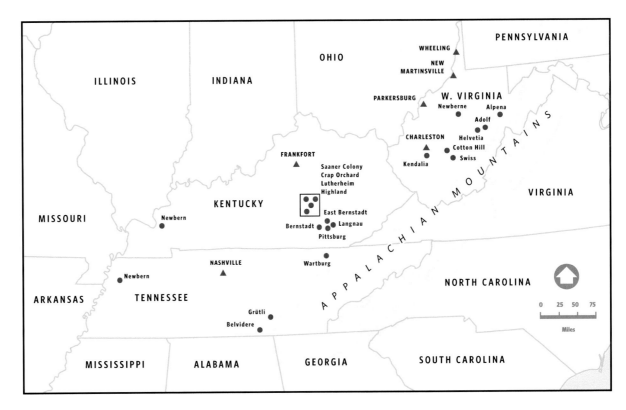

As news of the Swiss and the availability of land in Kentucky spread, however, more Swiss began to trickle into the state. In 1881, six families from Saanen in the Bernese Oberland established the Saaner Colony in Lincoln County. They were joined by eight additional families from the same area, and the "clustering" of various small groups of families emerged as a hallmark of the Swiss migration to the Appalachians.[14] Two years later, Jacob Ottenheim,

a land speculator from New York City, started the settlement of Crab Orchard in Lincoln County. Through land offices in New York and Louisville, he attracted ninety Swiss, German, and French families to the site. Realizing the problems of settling in an isolated area, he wisely supplied funds for a church, schoolhouse, rail station, and sawmill. By 1885 the settlement contained 150 families. They clustered in various locations on the large tract of land, forming the communities of Lutherheim and Highland, Kentucky. Several other families settled in surrounding counties, such as a small group at Langnau, founded by J. Leuenberger of Langnau, Switzerland. By 1890, these various aggregations of Swiss numbered 1,892, including 900 who lived in the more urban setting of Louisville.[15]

In Tennessee, Swiss settlements were founded in much the same way. The primary settlement of Grütli, in Grundy County, began in 1869, with the backing of a German investor, E. H. Plumacher, and the Swiss consul in Washington, D.C., John Hitz Jr. Their agent, Peter Staub, purchased twenty-five square miles of mountain wilderness and endeavored to resell it to immigrants.[16] Those who arrived first at the site found nothing but acres of timberland and one crude cabin intended to house three families until they could build their own homes. Many were discouraged, but a few stayed and slowly developed a small settlement. By 1886, the village numbered 330 Swiss and 70 native Tennesseeans.[17] Additional families filtered into Tennessee during the next two decades, forming the communities of Wartburg in Morgan County and New Berne in Deyer County. Small concentrations of Swiss also lived in the mining town of South Pittsburg, Marion County, and in the Belvidere section of Franklin County, Tennessee.

As in the case of Kentucky, Swiss who moved to Tennessee did not always come directly from Switzerland. In fact, they very often migrated south from Ohio, Pennsylvania, New York, Indiana, Illinois,

and Iowa. Individual families tended to aggregate in one locale in response to advertising campaigns and letters from relatives. However, land purchases made over a decade or two, on thousands of acres usually led to very decentralized communities. Clusters of families separated by distance and topography formed scattered rural neighborhoods, as one-room schools, kinship relationships, and economic ties developed between them. The rural regions in Tennessee never attracted great numbers from Europe or the United States. By 1890, the Swiss population in Tennessee was 1,027, four hundred sixty of whom lived in Memphis and Nashville.[18]

The movement of Swiss immigrants into the interior of West Virginia followed a similar pattern. One or two initial settlements were established through the use of advertising and propaganda. Later, individual families filtered in, settling nearby and forming their own small groups. Before mountain villages like Helvetia were settled, Swiss were present in several West Virginia towns along the Ohio River, such as Parkersburg, New Martinsville, and Wheeling. They organized various cultural clubs and enjoyed wide participation in community affairs. One of them, Mr. C. C. Egerter from Bern, served as mayor of Wheeling, Captain of the Harbor, and U.S. customs officer during his lifetime.[19] From these centers on the Ohio, a few Swiss families ventured south and east into the Kanawha River Valley, eventually following the watershed into the interior mountains along the New and Gauley Rivers. Unfortunately, very little is known about these tiny groups. In 1881, settlements were reported at Cotton Hill, a small railroad stop on the New River, just upstream of Hawks Nest, and at Kendalia on Blue Creek, in Kanawha County. Kendalia was founded by a few families from Schaffhausen, Switzerland, who maintained well-managed farms and started vineyards. Access to the area, however, was poor, and the settlement must have had a short life. Topographic surveys done in 1895 showed only one building on the site.[20] In the same general area, the village of Swiss on the Gauley River, in Nicholas County, was the center for five Swiss families who moved there in 1870. They reportedly took over abandoned farms in the area and developed them with skill and success. Eventually the community became known as "Swiss" by common consent. West Virginia, it seems, was even less attractive than Kentucky and Tennessee. In 1890, people of Swiss origin in the state totaled only 610.[21]

The most concentrated settlements were in Randolph County, where Helvetia was founded by five families in 1869. Its establishment led to the migration of several hundred people and a chain of three new communities. Events at Helvetia were typical of those recorded at the settlements in Kentucky and Tennessee. Speculative land dealings prevailed, making the pioneer venture more difficult than it already was; immigrants were attracted primarily from northern and western states, with some coming directly from Europe; the settlers were predominantly German Swiss, Protestant, and often from the canton of Bern; and they settled in clusters throughout the mountains, creating decentralized communities. Under these circumstances, the Swiss settlements in the Appalachians developed some distinctive characteristics. Compared to Swiss colonies in the Midwest, they were poorly planned and loosely organized. The colony of New Glarus in Green County, Wisconsin, for example, was founded by a single group of immigrants who came from Switzerland together, for the express purpose of settling in the same community. A search party purchased good land in the name of the group, and they agreed on a charter with rules and regulations for the settlement of the new community. The members themselves controlled the acquisition of land according to the provisions of the charter. As a result, the population was centralized, and the community highly structured in its early years. Its geographic location made farming relatively easy and placed it near to developing markets.[22] The Appalachian settlements had none of these advantages. They struggled to survive and to maintain an agricultural and communal way of life against great odds. By studying the history of Helvetia from its founding through World War II, one sees more clearly the events and conditions that shaped the character of Swiss settlements in the Appalachians, and how the immigrants coped with their strange, new environment.

Chapter 2

Helvetia's Founding

THE VILLAGE OF HELVETIA is cradled in a tiny valley along the headwaters of the Buckhannon River, in the rugged, southwestern corner of Randolph County. Here, in the uppermost part of the watershed, the steep mountains and narrow valleys have for two centuries enforced a solitary way of life on their inhabitants. Although the best land in the broad Buckhannon River Valley (and neighboring Tygart Valley) was taken by the 1780s, the upper Buckhannon remained isolated and sparsely settled throughout most of the nineteenth century. The mountains imposed a prolonged pioneer environment on the few settlers willing to venture into this harsh domain.[1] The earliest white settlers, mostly English and Scotch-Irish, lived principally by hunting and gathering, growing corn, and grazing a few head of livestock on the natural vegetation. When

the first Swiss settlers arrived in 1869, the transition from this woods economy to a more diversified agrarian economy had not yet been made.[2] They found themselves in a beautiful but difficult environment, which challenged their most basic skills of survival and endurance.

The decision to move to such an isolated area was made by only a few. They were not attracted so much by the current conditions in the area as by its potential. Above all else, they wanted to live on the land, to maintain small, efficient farms and make their homes among people of the same cultural and linguistic background. The Appalachians were richer in natural resources than they had ever imagined, and they hoped to use these resources to build a future for themselves and their families. But if Helvetia was at first a vision, it was also an alternative—an alternative to wage labor in Europe and the United States; an alternative to the anonymity of urban immigrant life and pressures of rapid adjustment in a new and different culture. Certainly other locations in the United States would have offered the same hope and security, but during the 1870s and 1880s, advertising as astute as any modern Madison Avenue campaign drew attention to the central Appalachians. Large landowners and investors employed agents to expound the virtues of the region and sell their lands at large profits. People came to settle and invest their life savings, but most had no idea how difficult the next decade of their lives would be.

For the first group of Helvetia settlers, the move began as an opportunity to leave Brooklyn, New York, which after the Civil War was forced to absorb more and more foreign immigrants as their numbers increased daily through New York Harbor. By 1869 the Swiss were an established group of around 750 in Brooklyn, many of whom belonged to an association called the *Grütliverein*. The *Grütliverein* was, in essence, a mutual aid society organized to help its members and their families in the event of illness or death. Local societies could affiliate with the North American Grütli Alliance, a nationwide group which connected local chapters of Swiss Americans.[3]

In early 1869, a Swiss agent in New York offered a large tract of land in West Virginia for the consideration of *Verein* members who might like to farm their own property. The tract was being sold by Samuel A. Peugh and Samuel S. Smoot of Washington, D.C., who had earlier employed a Swiss surveyor named John B. Isler to map out their claim. Such a prospect was of considerable interest to the *Verein*, and it was decided that six of their members should investigate the possibilities of settlement. On October 15, 1869, Jacob Halder, Ulrich Müller, Henry Asper, Joseph Zielmann, Mathias Marti, and Xavier Holzweg set out from Brooklyn for Randolph County, West Virginia.[4]

It was a long and expensive trip by rail via Philadelphia, Baltimore, and then west over the Alleghenies to Clarksburg, West Virginia, the railroad station nearest their destination. Upon arrival, they found Clarksburg a small but thriving town of some 1,300 people. Informants at the local hotel told the men that the remaining sixty miles of their trip had to be made on foot or horseback through densely forested mountains, but this news did not deter their investigation. The next morning the all-male committee continued on foot by the prescribed route, heading south to Weston and then southeast to the post village of French Creek in Upshur County. As they passed through the small towns and settlements, the people were friendly to them. They observed that farming practices were not as sophisticated as in the northern states, but the West Virginians were obviously self-sufficient.[5]

From French Creek the men were pointed toward the tiny settlement of Selbyville, where they met the Right Fork of the Buckhannon River. They noted the fresh, clear water and the abundance of native trout as they crossed the narrow stream and started up the next mountain. The rough, dirt roads which they had been following up to now suddenly became little more than a footpath leading into the forest. The men were amazed by what they saw as they walked on. Tall hardwoods, four and five feet in diameter, lined the trail; around almost every turn was another species of wildlife. Squirrels hopped from tree to tree gathering chestnuts for the winter, while turkeys fed on the abundance of wild berries. The autumn leaves blowing in the breeze painted a colorful picture for them. It was indeed a beautiful land.

As they approached their destination, the trail led over a steep mountain, rising 700 feet in elevation from the river, then descended into a narrow valley on the Left Fork of Right Fork of the Buckhannon. Where the tiny riverlet, Upper Trout Run, met the fork, they found perhaps thirty acres of bottomland and beginnings of the survey made by their countryman, Isler. A few English settlers lived secluded in rough clearings in the upland area, but aside from these, the vicinity contained only large expanses of virgin timber, rushing brooks, and wild game. The land, the committee could report, while extremely isolated, was pristine.[6] As they looked around them, the men perceived a natural paradise.

As the band of men began their four-day hike back to Clarksburg, they talked of their impressions and shared their dreams. They envisioned pastures carved out of the forest, cows grazing on the hillsides, the smell of freshly cut timbers for new houses. With so many trees they would always have building materials and fires to keep them warm. They spoke also of a community where they would be free to carry on the language and traditions of their homeland. True, it was a wilderness, but it was a rich wilderness where a hardworking man could make a home for himself and his family.

Over the course of the trip the men had grown closer together. The trek was not unlike a field expedition they might have done in the Swiss military, and as they talked of the game they would shoot and the trees they would fell, a sense of vision and camaraderie developed among them. When they returned to Brooklyn some days later, they made a full report of their findings and ideas to the *Verein*. Here the many disadvantages as well as the immense possibilities were discussed, but no one was persuaded to make such a risky venture—no one, that is, except for five of the six men who had actually seen the land. All but Xavier Holzweg made immediate arrangements to purchase 100 acres at $5.00 per acre, and move their families at the beginning of winter, 1869. This vital mistake in timing created great hardships for the group and pointed to their lack of experience in pioneering and homesteading. The long trip and the first winter were nothing short of a gruesome survival experience. No lives were lost, but the ordeal was long remembered by those who lived through it.[7]

"I was the first woman settler to stay," said eighty-eight-year-old Marguerite Asper, as she recalled her journey for a newspaper reporter to the wilderness

Christian Bürki, a settler from
Canton Bern, Switzerland,
stands in a section of virgin
forest near Helvetia, c. 1890.
This environment of huge
hardwoods, hemlock, and
flowering rhododendron
impressed the search committee
on their trek to Randolph
County. Aegerter photo.

valley which became Helvetia, "but I always wanted to go back to New York. That was a place where you could enjoy life. But you see, I met Henry and as soon as we were married, we moved down here. At first I cried, and asked Henry to take me back to New York, but he would say, 'No, I want to live here, work here, and be buried here!' It was a cruel land and cruel work."[8]

Recalling the last sixty miles from the railstation, Mrs. Asper described one of the most bitter and frightening events of her life. "We were cold and tired," she remembered of the four-day trip. "I had never been on a horse before and begged Henry to let me walk while he rode and carried the baby, but he was afraid the deep snow and awful cold would make me sick." After growing up in Frankfurt am Main, and living in New York City for four years, she found the Appalachian backcountry a great shock. "It looked like a wilderness . . . ," she exclaimed, "there were always wild animals around our house; we often ate bear meat and our cow ran all day with the deer."[9]

The men and women who accompanied the Aspers must have felt much the same way those cold December days as they trudged through the snow toward an uncertain future. They had all met in Brooklyn after coming from various parts of Switzerland and Germany. Now they were tied together by a bond of friendship and necessity in their joint undertaking. In 1865 Jacob and Barbara Halder had immigrated to Rome, New York, from

their home in Lenzburg, Switzerland. The couple, now in their forties, had eleven children, only two of whom had come with their parents to the United States. During their short stay in New York three additional children were born, and through their affiliation with the Brooklyn *Grütliverein*, the family migrated to West Virginia. Mrs. Halder was pregnant with her fifteenth child as she made the trip over the mountains.[10]

By contrast, Joseph Zielmann ventured into the Appalachian wilderness a thirty-two-year-old, single farmer. Hatmaker, Mathias Marti, was accompanied by three Marti women, each listed as a housekeeper in the 1870 census. (The records do not disclose the exact relationships of the family members.) Ulrich and Mary Müller were forty-one and fifty years old when they decided to leave Brooklyn, and the Aspers themselves had two children, including Henry Jr., who was less than one year old when they made the trip. Together the total of eleven adults, five men and six women, had an average age of nearly thirty-eight years. All the men were born in Switzerland although, like Henry Asper, those who married in the United States sometimes chose wives from neighboring countries such as Germany or France. They formed a diverse combination of individuals whose hopes of a better life in America were not yet realized.[11]

When the travel-weary group arrived at the chosen location, " . . . a few trees carved out in the surrounding woods, a few cross roads or trails leading to the distant settlers," they found the tiny log cabin the men had built two months earlier during their investigation. It was their only shelter from the winter wind. "There was one room . . . the settlement house," Mrs. Asper recalled, "where fifteen of us lived for almost a year . . . We slept at night in beds nailed around the walls. A few days after we got here was the end of the year 1869, and we gathered in the settlement house to find a name for our new home. We all liked the name Helvetia, the old name for Switzerland, best of all those proposed." After properly christening their new community, they celebrated the New Year with German and Swiss songs and dances, as they would have in Europe, but such occasions were rare, Mrs. Asper hastened to add. "Most of the time we worked hard . . . I can remember chopping down trees in the moonlight."[12]

As earlier settlers to the Appalachians had done, the Swiss cut down the huge trees and planted corn in the clearings, but the skills of clearing and hunting were not initially their strong points.[13] They learned the various methods from local West Virginians and by trial and error. Within a short time their skills of fishing, hunting, and gathering other foods from the forest improved greatly. They seldom went hungry, although it was necessary to develop a taste for bear meat and other wild game.

The first winter passed slowly for the Brooklyn group, but as the spring sun began to warm the valley, the weary settlers put most of the difficulties of winter behind them. Clearing and planting began early, and the children played outdoors, making life in the one-room cabin much easier. Almost six months after their arrival, as the fresh weather of May brought lush, green foliage to the forest, the settlers were visited by a distinguished-looking stranger, a fellow Swiss who had been in the United States some thirty years. Karl Lutz was an amiable, middle-aged man whose arrival marked a turning point in the life of the settlement.[14]

The settlers did not know that forty years earlier Karl E. Lutz had been an employee of the Bernese government until he was forced to leave the country. An engineer by trade, Lutz had risen quickly to the position of *Kantonal Baumeister*, or state architect, by his late twenties. He had owned an expensive home in the capital city of Bern, had friends in the government, and enjoyed what might have been a bright future, until he was convicted of a serious felony.[15] In 1832, Lutz had been appointed the inspector of public works projects in the canton, and part of his new position was to oversee the dismantling of the old city wall around Bern. The blocks were to be sorted and the good stones sold in order to save money and materials. All went well until he was accused of embezzling money from the sale of stones and of not forwarding various payments to fellow workers. He also failed to turn in receipts and accurately report expenditures for his travels around the canton to inspect the numerous building projects. [16]

Margaretha Asper and son Henry Jr. about 1925, fifty-five years after their journey from Brooklyn, New York, to Helvetia. Their small cabin, now with wood siding and fitted with windows, is in the background. Photographer unknown.

A five-month investigation ensued in which both the cantonal government and the public works department became involved. When Lutz came to trial in 1840, the court found him guilty of embezzlement and sentenced him to five years in prison. He was also ordered to pay back the stolen money, a total of SF 5,026.28 (SF = Swiss Francs) with 5 percent interest, in addition to court costs and travel expenses. [17] In a panic, his many creditors demanded payment, and the ex-inspector's debts suddenly rose to SF 42,195 (the equivalent is approximately SF 800,000 today, or $815,000). Finding it impossible to pay such a large sum, Lutz sold his home and property, the total of which covered only half of the enormous debt. [18] Before he could be imprisoned, however, Lutz fled to the United States. He reappeared as Charles Lutz in Jeffersonville, New York, where he reportedly swindled several fellow Swiss and again escaped the jail keeper by breaking bail and moving to Scranton, Pennsylvania. He later moved to West Virginia, where he employed himself as a carpenter, and having been told of the recent arrival of Swiss settlers, he traveled to Helvetia to deliver an unpleasant message. [19]

Upon arriving at the settlement house, he explained to the families in their native dialect that the titles to their land were worthless. He contended that the land on which they stood belonged not to them, nor to Samuel Peugh from whom they had bought it, but to a West Virginia lawyer and politician living in Weston, West Virginia, named Jonathan M. Bennett.

What the settlers now discovered was that in November 1868, one year before their arrival, Samuel Peugh had lost his claim to land on the headwaters of the Buckhannon River. Peugh's claim was based on surveys made in the 1790s by Standish Forde and patented in 1800 under James Monroe, then governor of Virginia. Initially, it covered some 45,976 acres in present day Randolph, Upshur, and Webster Counties. [20] Later, in 1850, a portion of the same land was patented by Weeden Hoffman, David Bennett, and Jonathan M. Bennett living in Lewis County, (West) Virginia. In the 1860s, these men and their heirs succeeded in securing a legal title to at least 4,180 acres of Peugh's claim. Evidence suggests that Peugh was unaware of this action when he sold portions of the land to the Swiss settlers in 1869. [21] However, as a result of this chaotic land system, the settlers now faced

voided deeds and the possibility of losing everything they had worked for. Under the circumstances, they had little additional income with which to pay the legal owner. Shocked and saddened by this turn of events and not fluent enough in English to handle the crisis alone, they readily accepted Lutz's offer to work on their behalf in resolving the situation. [22]

During the summer Lutz had much of the area around Helvetia resurveyed, and determined that several prominent West Virginia landholders would be affected by the settlement. The central owner, Jonathan M. Bennett (1816 - 1887) was well known in the state as a previous delegate to the Virginia General Assembly, as well as a lawyer and land speculator who managed his investments through a controlling interest in the Bank of Weston. Two of Bennett's close associates also owned land in the area. Gidean D. Camden (1805–1901), a Clarksburg lawyer who served for many years as circuit court judge and state senator, was a noted land and oil speculator in the state. Another was Camden's nephew, John S. Hoffman (1821–1887), also an attorney who specialized in land titles and litigations. To those could be added a variety of smaller landowners, lawyers, and speculators who at one time owned land in the settlement vicinity. Together, this group represented some of the wealthiest and most powerful men in West Virginia at the time. They were the people, particularly Camden and Bennett, with whom the settlers now had to deal. [23]

The following weeks were very tense in the settlement as the problems of land ownership and prices were considered by both sides. Lutz cleverly suggested to the landholders that if the settlers were allowed to stay, more immigrants like them could be attracted. By subdividing their huge tracts into one- or two-hundred-acre plots, the lawyer-speculators could make a profit on their wilderness holdings and everyone would benefit. He also asked Bennett for permission to sell his land in the area and to become the agent for promoting immigration from Switzerland. Apparently unaware of Lutz's criminal record, Bennett and several of the other landholders readily agreed to the suggestion, hoping to develop their Randolph County lands into a profitable venture. [24] The settlers were offered their 100-acre plots for $1.50 per acre, with an arrangement to pay in biannual installments at 10 percent interest, over a period of three years. This was significantly less that the $5.00 per acre which they had earlier agreed to pay Peugh, and hoping to avoid further problems, four of the five families accepted the offer. Henry Asper remained firm in his thinking that Peugh was actually the rightful owner and that Lutz was a charlatan. In a letter to Bennett, Lutz said that Asper was causing a "great disturbance," and "shows himself as a bad and mean character. He wrote to New York and elsewhere about how bad it was here. He says that I was nothing but a Humbuger, liar and rascal &c, and that he would show me if I had the right to sell land . . ." [25] This clash with Asper was the first of many Lutz would have with the settlers. This one he was able to contain. Asper continued to try to discredit him

for several months, but when faced with a lawsuit for slander and possible eviction from his property, he apologized and paid a second time for the land. In this manner the problem was settled, and Charles Lutz, himself, became a member of the new community as its land agent and promoter. [26]

Lutz's initial plans for the settlement were straightforward and rational. If Helvetia were to be a growing, profitable village, he reasoned, it needed more people and more capital. Toward this end, he approached Bennett and Hoffman for seed money to recruit immigrants in Switzerland and to build a much needed sawmill in the community. The landholders, however, were unwilling to invest any money in the project. In May 1871, they refused him money for a European trip, and as late as 1873, the first sawmill was still incomplete. [27] On this point, Bennett's biographer, Harvey M. Rice, misunderstood his role in Helvetia's founding. Rice wrote that the planting of immigrants at Helvetia "realized a dream that he [Bennett] had entertained for many years." While it is true that Bennett advertised his land in Germany and elsewhere, profitable sale of real estate was his primary motive. Once the settlement was founded, he refused to support its development in any way. Nor, as Rice states, did Bennett ever finance Lutz's travel to Europe. The newly-appointed agent was left entirely to his own devices. [28]

With no cash to travel abroad, Lutz worked at drawing potential migrants from the adjoining

Helvetia, Randolph Co., West Virginien.

Die Colonie Helvetia, Randolph County, West Virginien, wurde im October 1871 in Angriff genommen. Für Alle, die sich dafür interessiren, ist Gutes und Böses zu wissen wie folgt:

Auf der Karte ersichtlich, liegt West Virginien zwischen dem 38sten und 40sten Grade von Nord nach Süd, und Randolph County speciell unterm 39sten Grad. Vermittelst dieser geographischen Lage ist West Virginien kein südlicher und kein nördlicher Staat, sondern hält die goldene Mitte. Hier weiß man nichts von extremer Hitze, noch Kälte. Der Schnee lag letzten Winter nie über 8 Zoll hoch, bei noch keine 2 Zoll tief gefrorenem Boden. Die Sommer sind lang und nicht übermäßig heiß, die Winter kurz und mild. Unter solchen Umständen ist nicht zu wundern, wenn sich das hiesige Klima als eines der gesundesten herausstellt. Gastrische- und Lungenkrankheiten des Nordens, sind eben so unbekannt als sämmtliche Fieber des Westens und Südens. So ist auch das außerordentliche Durchschnittsalter der West Virgi-

Um, von Ferne kommend, sich hier anzusiedeln und nicht in drückende Nahrungssorgen zu verfallen, muß man über ungefähr $200 bis $300 zu verfügen haben, nachdem Fracht- und Reisekosten, nebst e r s t e r Bezahlung für's Land, abgerechnet sind. Wer das hat und kann dann bei solchem Clima, Boden, Wasser und Holz, bei gesundem Verstand, geraden Knochen und Thätigkeitssinn, nicht vorankommen, d. h. nicht schnell und sicher sich eine glückliche Heimath schaffen, der suche dann den Fehler nirgend anderswo, als bei sich selbst.

Für Jagdliebhaber ist ein ausgedehnt reiches Feld. Bär, Hirsch, Truthahn voran, eine Menge kleineres Wild nachfolgend. Es heißt, hin und wieder zeigen sich Klapperschlangen. Seit 3 Jahren immer im Walde lebend, sah ich in der Colonie Helvetia noch kein solches Thier, gewiß ein Beweis, daß sie selten sind; außer diesem Ungeziefer ist hier kein einziges Thier zu fürchten, denn die Bären fliehen jedes Kind. Die kleinen Flüsse sind voll der schmackhaftesten Forellen mit röthlichen Fleische, doch fängt man sie selten über

states. In early 1871, he reported that he had spent $60 of his own money in an effort to recruit a dozen men from Ohio who later did not come for fear of bad land titles. Another man, "a Pennsylvanian of some influence," had planned to invest in Helvetia, but backed out for the same reason. [29] Thus, the first attempts to find willing immigrants for the settlement failed. Throughout 1871 the would-be agent had very little income and resorted to asking Bennett and Camden for money on several occasions. They always refused. [30]

During 1872, however, the flow of settlers increased, largely due to Lutz's publication of flyers and newspaper advertisements about the settlement. As an immigrant himself, Lutz knew how to reach potential migrants. His clever ads offered "splendid virgin forests," sold at the "ridiculous price of $3.00 per acre," and a climate which "followed the golden middle." The hills, he said in one

publicity flyer, "are full of the best coal and iron ore . . . the minerals, along with the magnificent wood, will bring us railroads in all directions before the end of the decade," [1870s]. Although many of his statements were half-truths, or proved to be false, the ads were effective in bringing new settlers to Helvetia—so effective, in fact, that he hired a surveyor named James Pickens to lay out the new tracts. Pickens was a local landowner who would eventually carve out his own town just five miles from Helvetia. But for the moment, he became Lutz's much-needed employee and associate in the land business. [31]

The landholders gave Lutz only the most general guidelines by which to sell land. They asked from $1.50 to $2.00 per acre and reserved the right to hold all deeds until payment was received. Jonathan Bennett offered Lutz 10 percent of income from land which he sold. Feeling the market would bear more, however, Lutz persuaded Bennett to keep the entire $2.00 per acre and allow him to add a commission of $1.00 per acre for his costs. [32] By adding that commission to the price of the land, Lutz boosted his profits to a full 33 percent of the total cost. This amounted to a substantial income when, in 1872, he sold approximately 1,650 acres of Bennett's property, and kept for himself an equal number of dollars. This same land sold at Bennett's original 10 percent would have brought the agent only $330.00. [33] These and other sales, increased the agent's income dramatically, and with a new sense of assurance, he asked to marry Rachel McCartney, the daughter of a local West Virginia farmer. Rachel was forty-eight years younger than her new husband, but she was distantly related to Jonathan M. Bennett— a fact which Lutz did not fail to mention. "She is a far relation of you, and a splendid wife for me," Lutz wrote, "she is only twenty years old, but no matter, I am man enough for her." [34]

While Lutz was busy currying Bennett's favor, his credibility with the settlers was being undermined by his unusual and awkward business practices. He normally took the commission from the first payment, then instructed the immigrants to pay the balance directly to the landholders. By 1873 the increased number of small buyers made it difficult for the landholders to manage so many accounts in their otherwise busy lives. Thus, with their permission, Lutz began the practice of collecting all the monies and forwarding them to the landholders only after the last payment arrived. [35] This most recent twist gave Lutz the role of bill collector, credit agency, and in effect, banker. He had to keep track of when payments were due, hold money in escrow until all payments were in, and then deliver it to the landholders. During the entire time between the first and last payments, the buyer had no legal document to show that the land he had paid for belonged to him. This new policy, coupled with the inability of the settlers to get deeds quickly and directly, brought the land agency, if not the landholders themselves, into question. It also put Lutz into a perfect position to misuse or embezzle money in escrow. [36]

This dubious procedure went unchecked until Lutz began to exploit its loopholes. In 1873, the tiny community added a physician to its ranks, Dr. Christian F. Stucky. Stucky was a contemporary of Lutz's, having graduated from the University of Bern Medical School in 1847, just a few years after Lutz had fled the country. Moving to Helvetia from Ohio, Stucky dealt with the agent for a piece of property in the usual way, making the community his home and area of practice. One year elapsed when, according to Lutz, Stucky had not made payment on his land. Feeling no more obligations, Lutz used the fact that the doctor had no deed to resell the property to another settler, Jakob Gobeli. Angered by such underhandedness, Stucky soon became one of Lutz's greatest antagonists. In the following months, he led an effort to oust Lutz from his position as land agent. [37]

His efforts were only briefly interrupted during the summer of 1874 when Lutz traveled to Switzerland to attempt the full-scale publicity project he initially intended. Financing the trip himself, he sailed at the end of May leaving his colleague and surveyor James Pickens in charge. In a brief letter from Bern he indicated to Bennett that he planned to bring back his nephew, Eugene Lutz, and two sons of his "cousin and friend Mr. Schenk, the actual President of the Republic of Switzerland." The trip, he predicted, would be of "great consequences" for the state. [38] The young men did, in fact, immigrate. Eugene Lutz lived in Helvetia for a short time, but by 1878 had joined Charles Mylius (another Swiss), as a partner in a dry goods store in Buckhannon, West Virginia. The Schenk brothers settled on Turkeybone Mountain, about eight miles from Helvetia. They found the area difficult to farm and their frequent requests for money from home amused some of the more seasoned immigrants at Helvetia. No doubt quite disappointed in their elder cousin, who had brought them so far for such little opportunity, the brothers soon moved away. Paul, who held a graduate degree in agronomy, joined Otto Brunner to found the settlement of Bernstadt, Kentucky, in 1880. [39]

Lutz returned to Helvetia in late September 1874 to begin where he had left off. If any progress had been made in Europe toward directing emigrants to Helvetia, it was soon thwarted by his enemies in the community. While he was away, Dr. Stucky had persuaded James Pickens to sell him a parcel of land on Turkeybone Mountain. Discovering this, Lutz again tried to evict the doctor and sell the property to someone else. [40] By now it was not difficult to find supporters for taking action against the agent. A committee of twenty-six settlers joined Stucky in requesting that the landholders investigate Lutz's business practices. The group accused him of embezzling money which he collected in payment for land, and charged that he cheated settlers such as Stucky, causing them to lose their homes. As the situation heated up, Lutz wrote to Bennett hoping to diffuse it. "They will send delegates to you . . . for to inquire. Now please post them roughly, that's all I want. I am not safe for my life, but no matter, I think it is Ropes enough in the U.S. for to hang them, if I get killed—." [41]

Bennett and the other landholders preferred to avoid the adverse publicity of an open investigation, and when the committee found them aloof and unsupportive, they called on John Hitz Jr., the Swiss Consul General in Washington, D.C. Particularly interested in the case, Hitz traveled personally to Helvetia during the summer of 1875. He filed an extensive report on his visit and investigation which indicated an in-depth and balanced review of the matters. While praising Lutz for his early assistance to the Brooklyn group of settlers, he concluded that the agent conducted affairs which "defy any reasonable rules of business," and suggested that Lutz's services should have been offered without the charge of a commission. Hitz also criticized the landholders for "using" Lutz, not giving him "any substantial degree of trust," and ignoring the need for "correct and lawful surveying." This was, in fact, an accurate assessment. [42] From his visit, Hitz saw that the recent strife was tearing at the seams of the young settlement. He wrote that the Swiss in Helvetia were "unusually intelligent," and that if they would follow the path of "brotherly kindness and cooperation," the old proverb *Eintract macht stark* or "harmony makes strong," would find great value in the community. [43]

The fighting was not over, however, and harmony was far from the doorstep. The investigation committee called a community meeting where Lutz rebutted the various charges at length, and attempted to persuade the group of about fifty men to publish that he was innocent of all accusations. "At once the great majority were ready to do so immediately," Lutz said, "but Stucky arose, warning them not to do so; finally a great quarrel ensued of which the result was that a committee of seven should investigate once more if I committed fraud, that this meeting should report to a general meeting, and according to the report the settlers would act." [44]

Exactly what the local committee concluded will probably never be known, but it is clear that by September 1877, Lutz realized that he had been undone. His credibility had been destroyed, the flow of settlers had ceased, and neighbors had

Letter from C. E. [Karl] Lutz to J. M. Bennett, 26 July 1874. Reporting on his trip to Switzerland to advertise Helvetia, Lutz notes in the postscript that he has persuaded two sons of the Swiss president to return with him. Jonathan M. Bennett Collection, West Virginia and Regional History Collection.

become enemies. Unable to gain support from the landholders, he wrote them that he was planning to leave Helvetia. "I have to leave here most naked with my wife and two children. Old as I am [73] I am not able to work at my trade anymore. I am bound to search somewhere for employment." [45] In April 1878 the banished land agent sold his house for $1,200. He attempted to shock Bennett by writing that he was destined to the poorhouse and was contemplating suicide. He begged for money from both Camden and Bennett during 1878 and asked for their help in obtaining a job. During this time, Bennett gave his power of attorney to James Pickens, refusing to have anything more to do with Charles Lutz. [46]

Lutz, however, was more resilient than anyone expected. In late 1878 he moved with his family to Beverly, West Virginia, then the seat of Randolph County. There, with the support of local lawyers and land speculators, he petitioned the West Virginia legislature to fund his work in bringing immigrants to the state. This, along with help from political connections, brought Lutz a windfall he could never have expected in Helvetia. The following year he was appointed Immigration Officer for the entire state of West Virginia. Under the legitimacy of this new title, he succeeded in bringing some twenty families directly from Switzerland for a new settlement he dubbed Alpine, located between the Shavers and Glady Forks of Cheat River.* Having been promised good farmland, the immigrants were very disappointed with the wilderness territory. They presented a petition asking for the governor of the state to take some action against Lutz, but as in Helvetia, their efforts failed to achieve results. [47]

Finding himself quite unpopular in Alpine, Lutz again changed directions to work on a similar plan for selling land on the Middle Fork River. An agent sent to Switzerland led a group of thirty

immigrants to the newly contrived community of West Huttonsville, later renamed Adolph. The following events unfolded much as they had at Alpine and Helvetia, and Lutz soon departed the scene, leaving the tiny communities to fend for themselves. Sometime in the mid-1880s, he left West Virginia for New York, where he died on the fifth of November, 1887, at the age of eighty-two years. [48]

In Helvetia, a committee of seven settlers headed by the local pastor, Franz Münzner, assumed the task of encouraging immigration. They were elected, they said, to supervise real estate, examine deeds for the buyers, and recommend to newcomers the easiest travel and transport possible. The committee published its own modest publicity flyer announcing that the land swindle, "that fearful ghost to which so many fell victim . . .," had been cleared away. "We have here a group from the whole settlement whose task is to help all new arrivals," the committee wrote, hoping to counter some of the adverse publicity the settlement had received. [49]

Charles Lutz was not soon forgotten, however. He was remembered as an opportunist who understood the fine line between illegal and unethical behavior. He worked with the consent and, for some years, the backing of expert lawyers and judges who profited from the land he sold. An immigrant himself, he understood the strengths and weaknesses of the immigrant situation and used them to his advantage. He was most influential with

---

*   Today the spelling is anglicized to Alpena.

Swiss Germans because he spoke their language, and he took advantage of their relatively small knowledge of English to deny them full access to the legal system which they so desperately needed. Consequently, he was able to threaten them with lawsuits for which they had no money or experience.

During his eight-year career in Helvetia, Lutz was directly or indirectly responsible for the migration of about 350 people to the community. A small portion came directly from Europe, but most migrated from other parts of the United States. His impressive advertisements, offering splendid conditions for settlement, drew his reader's attention and acted as a catalyst in the decision-making process. But moving was not something that was taken lightly. A single advertisement or a speech by a traveling agent was seldom enough to get a family to move. Social and economic conditions, as well as the values and aspirations of the immigrants, were also key factors. By advertising in the urban, industrial areas of Ohio, Lutz targeted immigrants who were subject to the uncertainties and drudgeries of industrial life, or who had taken any available job in order to get established. In the anthracite regions of Pennsylvania, where working conditions were poor and labor unrest common, he likewise often found a receptive audience. General economic trends in the country were used to his advantage. A publicity campaign during the Panic of 1873 resulted in 84 new settlers in Helvetia, and an additional 133 in 1874. This was the largest influx of

people to the community in any two-year period of its history. [50]

The great majority of these had been single-family immigrants, who had come for Europe without the aid of an immigration society or the security of moving as part of a colony. They sought, as most nineteenth-century immigrants did, to live among people whose language and traditions were familiar. Much of Helvetia's attraction was the opportunity to live among other Swiss and Germans, to help build a new community in the seclusion of the mountains. [51]

Although farmland in Helvetia was generally of poor quality, the unspoiled nature of the land held attraction. The first immigrants from Brooklyn had been favorably impressed by their visit and investigation of natural resources. They, and those who followed them, clearly wanted to own land and work small, efficient farms. These things were dear to the Swiss and Germans and were very much respected in their societies. The area was far removed from economic centers, but it promised development and seemed to provide opportunity for the kinds of agricultural, communal, and small village commerce they knew and valued.

Helvetia was, in fact, built upon these hopes and dreams, although its birth involved a difficult and painful labor. It involved not only vision, courage, and endurance, but also misjudgments and bad luck. The first immigrant families found themselves in a survival situation, where tensions ran high, but friendships also ran deep. By 1880, it was clear that Helvetia would survive and that its people were beginning to create a new and secure place to live. Although the settlement had a distinctly European character, the settlers came in search of an American dream—their common motivation expressed through a proverb that the new land committee penned in bold letters at the close of its flyer: "EIGNER HERD IST GOLDES WERTH!," meaning literally, "One's own hearth is like gold!" [52]

Building the New Community

By 1875, Helvetia and its surroundings had reached a population of 381 immigrants and the number increased to 407 by 1880. To this initial group of Swiss and Germans fell the task of building a town and community where none had previously existed.[1] It was an endeavor very similar to pulling oneself up by the bootstraps, but in spite of the numerous pitfalls encountered throughout the 1870s, the settlers were able to create an enduring human and physical community. This was possible, in part, because a close interdependence was necessary to their survival and because they arrived with the practical ingenuity, physical health and stamina, and the desire to succeed. Although unversed in the particular techniques of homesteading, they brought a vast knowledge of wood and metalworking, stonemasonry, dairying, gardening, and other skills which were soon in use making homes and farms. This, combined with the plentiful resources and a healthy population, allowed the building of a unique Swiss American town.

The immigrants' new homes and associations reflected their cultural backgrounds as well as the demands of a wilderness setting. The rugged landscape, for example, dictated the location of pastures and meadows, the types of building materials available, and often the distance to a neighbor's house, while old world ideas and customs continued to influence their interaction with those same neighbors. At the outset they were a group of strangers, a collection of individual families who came with a variety of linguistic traditions, beliefs, and prejudices that could have easily splintered the settlement. These differences were themselves

Katherine and Johannes Hofer Sr. on their porch at Helvetia, 1903. The Hofers immigrated from Grosshöchstetten, Canton Bern in the early 1870s. Photo by Gottlieb Hofer.

reflections of the Swiss cultural landscape in the nineteenth century.

Switzerland is a small country, even by European standards, but its many valleys, terraces, and mountain passes harbor an immense variety of cultural traditions. The diversity is reflected, in part, by the number of language groups in the country. The Swiss federal government recognizes four national languages—German, French, Italian, and Ro-mansch. The most widely spoken, *Schwyzerdütsch*, or the Swiss dialect of German is the language of well over one-half of the citizenry. This linguistic plurality is complicated by countless dialects, none of which conform to any standard but their own, all of which are spoken with local pride.[2]

Of the Swiss who moved to Helvetia more than half originated in the German-speaking canton of Bern. They came primarily from small, lowland villages such as Langnau, Blumenstein, Münsingen, and Grosshöchstetten, and from hamlets in the Berner Oberland such as Boltigen and Schönried. A few originated in the city of Bern, but most were from rural areas where farming and trades were the main occupations. Their various Bernese dialects were the most frequently heard versions of *Schwyzerdütsch* in Helvetia, but there were also many others. At a time when the great majority of Swiss continued to live in the town of their birth, among people who had known their families for generations, Helvetia became a kind of German Swiss melting pot and microcosm of German Swiss emigration. Ranking after Bern, as frequent places of origin, were eleven other cantons, including Zürich, St. Gallen, Aargau, Baselland, and Appenzell a/R, (the primary cantons of origin), with Luzern, Glarus, Schaffhausen, Solothurn, Neuenberg, and Graubünden less represented in the community. Settlers from all these localities, including German families who came almost exclusively from the provinces of Saxony and Baden, were suddenly side

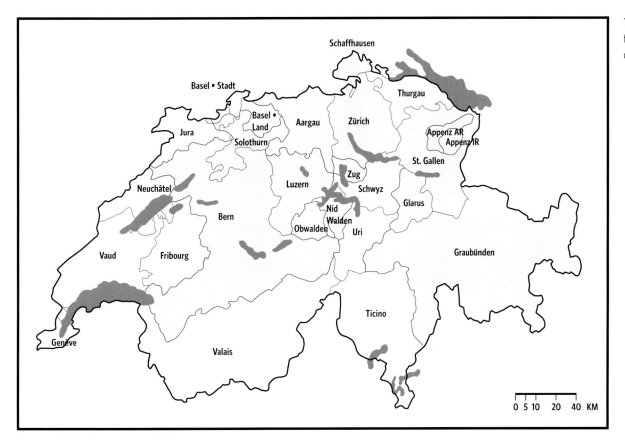

Schaffhausen

Basel • Stadt

Thurgau

Basel •
Land

Aargau

Zürich

Appenz AR
Appenz IR

Jura

Solothurn

St. Gallen

Neuchâtel

Luzern

Zug

Schwyz

Glarus

Bern

Nid
Walden

Obwalden

Uri

Graubünden

Vaud

Fribourg

Ticino

Genève

Valais

0 5 10   20   40 KM

The Swiss cantons (shaded) from which Helvetia immigrants originated.

by side in Helvetia. Although they all spoke a variety of German, dialectical differences could make it difficult to understand one's next-door neighbor.[3]

To the local English speakers the settlers were all simply "Dutchmen," but among themselves their differences in regional culture, religion, and language were quite apparent. The contrasts were most obvi-

ous between the German families, who were primarily Catholic, and the Swiss Protestants who formed the majority. Since the Reformation in Europe, relations between Swiss Catholics and Protestants had been hostile. As late as the 1840s Switzerland was polarized in a war between Catholic and Protestant sections. If all the prejudices of the homeland had

The Friedrich Bürki family at
their home near Helvetia, c.
1905. Born in Münsingen, Canton
Bern, Friedrich immigrated with
his parents in 1869, as did his
wife, Elisa Dubach. The two were
married at Helvetia in 1888.
Aegerter photo.

prevailed, community life would have been frag-
mented rather than supportive. In their new circumstances, however, the settlers were forced to put aside
some of their prejudices against other cantons, religious groups, and countries in order to forge a workable community. Certainly, biases remained, but
as a minority in a foreign country, their situation

required cooperation. The wilderness became a great
equalizer, serving to de-emphasize social differences and challenging the settlers to overcome what
could have been a stumbling block in building their
new community. The fact that the settlers advertised
the community in 1877 with no stipulations indicated their openness in accepting Swiss or German,

The Gottlieb Fahrner family on their mountain top farm, c. 1900. Fahrner immigrated from Zürich in 1857, settled in Davenport, Iowa, served in the Civil War, and moved his family to Helvetia in 1873. Aegerter photo.

Protestant or Catholic immigrants. [4] Nonetheless, the majority of the settlers were of Swiss stock and Protestant faith, and they, more than any other group, shaped the character of the developing settlement. They clung to their cultural identity, founded the primary institutions of the community, and established a Swiss identity for the community in the surrounding county and state. [5]

Of all the families that participated in this creative process, it is difficult to find one that could be

Some members of the Casper Metzener family at their home, c. 1912. Metzener and his wife Anna Schneitter (not shown) were married in Wengi, Canton Bern in 1857 and immigrated to Helvetia in 1882. Aegerter photo.

considered typical. The story of the Balthasar Merkli family, however, illustrates both the immigration patterns and the willingness to cooperate common to many of the settlers. Both Balthasar Merkli and his wife Franziska Bopp were born in Wettingen, Canton Aargau, Switzerland in the mid-1840s. Their families had lived in Wettingen for several generations, and by the late 1860s, young Balthasar was already an assistant foreman in a nearby spinning factory. His wife worked as a seamstress from her home.[6] Then in 1870, Merkli was offered the position of foreman, but without an increase in salary. He objected, and when the company refused to pay what he felt was a fair wage, he decided to emigrate to the United States. Later, when the firm agreed to pay the full foreman's wages, the young man would not give up his plans, even against the better judgment of his wife.[7]

The Merklis arrived in the United States at New York and moved to Cleveland, Ohio, where Franziska Merkli's brother lived. There, Balthasar learned to be a carpenter, and late in 1872 he heard of the need for builders in Helvetia. Picking up again, the family headed for West Virginia. They arrived in Clarksburg on November 1, 1872, where events showed how vulnerable to circumstances the immigrants were. During their overnight stay at Clarksburg, a local land broker persuaded them to forsake the idea of going to Helvetia and instead, move to an area on the Little Kanawha River in Gilmer County. This they would have done, if not for the chance meeting of a fellow Swiss who was going to Helvetia to meet her husband. Mrs. Anna Haslebacher implored the Merklis to accompany her on that last rugged four-day hike to Randolph County. Again changing their minds, the Merklis went on to Helvetia, where they lived for the next three months in the cold, drafty settlement house, while their own cabin was being built. [8]

The Merklis soon found that they were very different in at least one way from most of their neighbors. They

The Merklis in later life, c. 1915, with four of their six children. Their large wood-frame house in the background was a great improvement over the log settlement cabin. The family was originally from Wettingen, Canton Aargau. Aegerter photo.

were one of the very few Swiss Catholic families in the settlement. They decided, however, to attend the Reformed Church the settlers had organized, which they did until many years later when a Catholic church was built in the nearby town of Pickens. Extending their help in the community, they invited Helvetia's first Reformed pastor to live with them for three months until his house was completed. [9]

By these actions the Merklis showed that cooperation and compromise were important traits for living in the new community. Youth and good health, however, were also key elements in Helvetia's settlement. Without the ability to do long hours of hard physical labor, a family could not survive. Like the Merklis, the adults who chose to move to Helvetia were mainly married couples between the ages of

Portrait of Johannes Koprio from Canton Aargau. Koprio was an eccentric who spent much of his time playing the accordion and entertaining children with song and dance. He had no family in Helvetia and was cared for primarily by the church. Courtesy Mary Huber Marti.

twenty-five and forty-five. They were by now a select group, since they had already survived the most dangerous years of childhood diseases and arrived safely from an often hazardous passage across the Atlantic. Most had begun their families before arriving in Helvetia, and with continued births, children under the age of fifteen comprised 48.5 percent of the population in 1880. [10] According to their physician, Dr. Christian F. Stucky, the greatest threats to life, once in Helvetia, were typhoid fever, pneumonia, croup, and diphtheria. But those diseases, he said, were not as frequent as he had observed in other areas, and in most cases they were less severe. "In a twenty-seven year medical practice," the doctor reported to the Swiss consul, "I have never, proportionally speaking, seen less disease than here." [11]

Dr. Stucky's general observations are supported by statistics of life expectancy for a sample of Helvetia immigrants born between 1803 and 1868. In 1890, the average American male who was forty years old could expect to live 27.37 additional years. Helvetia males, however, could expect to live 31.59 additional years, or almost four years longer than average. For females the range was similar: U.S. – 28.76 years, Helvetia – 31.33 years. As a group, members of the Helvetia sample consistently showed a higher life expectancy at all ages between twenty and eighty than the general U.S. population of 1890. (See Appendix 4.) From this evidence it is clear that the settlers did arrive in good health, and that despite the difficult settlement years, they tended to remain healthy while living in the community. [12]

Johannes and Anna Teuscher moved to Helvetia in 1872 from Ohio. They were originally from Boltigen, Canton Bern, c. 1910. Aegerter photo.

The reasons for their good health can only be a matter of discussion since medical records for the immigrants do not exist. Dr. Stucky believed that the climate in West Virginia was an important factor, but this theory does not account for the immigrants' previous medical histories. Probably more important was a combination of complex factors including childhood care and nutrition, attention to sanitary conditions, and the increased chance of healthy people making it to Helvetia. For whatever exact reasons, the settlers were a vigorous group for whom the labor of pioneering was a physically healthful activity. [13]

Such a sturdy population began quickly carving out a home and future for itself. Within a few years of their arrival, the tall trees and

This drawing, probably done by settler Ulrich Müller and dated 1876, is the earliest surviving image of the new community. The artist was looking northeast into the village and drew just the central part of town. Center left, the Blum Sanatorium sat on the bank near the small one-room school. The sawmill puffed steam in the meadow and just ahead of the horse and wagon, on the right, was the general store. As land was cleared, new dwellings emerged from the wooded landscape. Courtesy of Gene and Anna Daetwyler. Redrawn for the author by Lorraine Duisit, 1979.

HELVETIA.
Randolph Co. West Virginia

fragrant laurel thickets that shaded the valley gave way to rough-hewn clearings. The meadow-line was pushed almost to the tops of the mountains surrounding the settlement, and farmers, taking advantage of the relatively level land, painstakingly cleared the tops of ridges. By 1876 about eighty acres had been cleared in the village alone. The huge logs, too numerous to use

This photo taken in the winter of c. 1895, clearly delineated the village lots in the central part of town. More land had been cleared since the 1870s and a number of new homes built, including the German Reformed Church overlooking the village in the right foreground. Courtesy Ruth Williamson.

and unsellable without a railroad to transport them, were rolled onto tremendous piles and burned. Working together, making use of what they could, the settlers hewed and notched the native hemlocks, poplars, and chestnuts to form one- and two-room log cabins. These provided the first temporary homes for the families until time and money allowed the building of more comfortable frame houses. [14]

As the settlers continued to clear the dense forest and to define the mountain landscape according to property boundaries, Helvetia began to take the shape of a mountain village. The layout for village properties was the design of Charles Lutz, who in the mid-1870s

Looking east, c. 1910, the village was older and more picturesque. The Star Band Hall was added in the front of the Daetwyler home, roads were improved, fruit trees matured, and hillside pasture was covered with thick grass. Clearing land for farm use reached its peak by this time. Aegerter photo.

subdivided his centrally located, 100-acre tract into about as many town lots. Lutz envisioned a tightly formed, self-sufficient community similar to Swiss alpine villages, where most of the trades and goods needed for daily life were at hand. With this in mind, he offered choice lots to craftsmen who would migrate to Helvetia. This approach was quite successful in the early years, and in addition to attracting skilled people, it determined the size and use of village properties for many years to come. Each of his small, rectangular lots fronted on the stream bisecting the valley, and a narrow dirt road meandered along the valley connecting the

Close-up view of the village center during a community event about 1910. The Star Band is in the foreground, with a horse-drawn "swing" or merry-go-round behind it to the left. Left to right along the dirt street is the Gottlieb Daetwyler home, Daetwyler's cobbler shop, and the community store. Aegerter photo.

various parcels. Viewed from one of the slopes a few hundred feet above, the developing settlement spread symmetrically along the course of the watershed for a distance of one to two miles in each direction. [15]

In many respects, the tiny valley harboring the settlement looked like countless other ravines in the highlands of West Virginia, but as well-built homes and shops began to dot the landscape and as backyards were cleared for gardens and pastures, it began to take on a separate character. Its intimate setting and way of life were unlike the lumber and coal towns which had sprung up around the state in the

View of the Blum Sanatorium
c. 1915, after it was converted
to a hotel owned and operated
by Herman Koerner. Aegerter
photo.

last century, nor did it resemble the centers of commerce which had been founded along the navigable rivers of the Mountain State. In these towns, industry and resource extraction were the key factors which often made living conditions dirty and bleak, and created long rows of houses along the railroad tracks or warehouses along the rivers. Helvetia, on the other hand, was not a company town, a boomtown, nor even a center of commerce; it was an isolated community of craftsmen and farmers whose main occupations became clearing and planting. Their daily lives followed the seasonal rhythms of nature, and the community came to reflect both their struggle and their harmony with it.

Thus, a visitor to the community in the years following 1880 would have discovered a rough-cut, but pleasant agricultural community, rationally laid out and inhabited by a variety of skilled people. By this time, Helvetia boasted some twenty different craftsmen and professionals from cheesemakers to clergymen, and from the standpoint of practical ingenuity, most were particularly well prepared to forge a new home. Among those who settled in the village proper were several men of distinctive skill and ambition. Most of them settled permanently in the community and contributed strongly to community life. A few others, however, moved away in a short time. Their ranks included two medical doctors, Dr. Christian F. Stucky, whose important role in the community has been noted, and Dr. Richard Blum. Blum came to Helvetia from Wheeling, West Virginia, to start a sanatorium for treating tuberculosis in the mountains. He built a large, Victorian-style resort house to board his patients, but when the venture failed to mature, he returned to Wheeling, leaving the large building to serve as a hotel and residence for many years to come. [16] Other shopkeepers along the village throughway included George Betz, a miller from Württemburg, Germany; August Vogel, a young Swiss settler who built the community's first steam-powered sawmill; Frank Huber, an enterprising blacksmith; and Gustavus Sennhauser, the first of a long line of village merchants. Like Blum, Sennhauser hoped his investment in Helvetia would be more profitable than it turned out to be. He moved to the community from New Philadelphia, Ohio, where he and associate Nicholas Kaderly owned a drygoods business. Speculating that Helvetia might be a good place to branch

Portrait of Margaret and Gustavus Sennhauser c. 1860. Sennhauser was Helvetia's first merchant and a founding member of the German Reformed Church, before moving back to New Philadelphia, Ohio in 1878. Courtesy Mary Huber Marti.

out, the men invested in several town lots and Sennhauser opened a general store. He soon became the postmaster and an active citizen in the community, but after seven years he decided to move his family back to Ohio for greater educational and economic opportunities. [17]

Also along the main village street stood the home and cobblershop of Gottlieb Daetwyler, a small man with kind eyes and a bushy beard, from the canton

Cobbler Gottlieb Daetwyler and wife Lena with their family about 1908. Aegerter photo.

of Aargau. He supported his large family by farming and by making and repairing shoes, although to obtain the necessary leather, he was forced to carry it on foot some fifty miles from Weston. Daetwyler typified those who remained in Helvetia their entire lives. He combined his craft with gardening and husbandry and was content with the prospects of a small, local business.[18]

In addition to these, the long list of Helvetia craftsmen included blacksmiths, tailors, bakers, wagonmakers, cheesemakers, and gardeners, but some of the most important craftsmen were carpenters and stonemasons. In a town with so much building, they were at a premium. Such people attracted to the area included stonemasons Ulrich Müller, Christian Zumbach, and Mathias Suesli, and carpenters Christof Schilling, Balthasar Merkli, Henry Eckhardt, and John Karlen. By the mid-1870s these men helped erect some twenty-six houses in the valley, causing the village center to develop rapidly.[19]

Although almost all the immigrants had strong vocational backgrounds, the size of the community could not support all their trades as businesses. This required that everyone farm in addition to whatever skilled training he may have had. Men set up as craftsmen in the village often bought adjacent hillside land upon which to grow crops, and others purchased farmland several miles away in order to graze animals or grow hay. Under the circumstances, the majority of people preferred to settle on the upland ridges surrounding the town, where the land better suited farming. This necessity alone meant that Helvetia became a decentralized community with the village as a nucleus. When the census taker arrived in the summer of 1880, he found only fifty-six people living in the village compared to more than 302 living on the surrounding mountaintops and in the countryside several miles away. Families found that their neighborhood consisted of adjacent landowners on a common ridge or valley, a total of perhaps five to seven families on six or seven hundred acres.

As the migration to Helvetia grew, various clusters of families began to emerge, forming scattered rural neighborhoods in the surrounding mountains. At the center of each was a one-room school. Haslebacher School was located on a ridge, central to many area farms, about two and one-half miles south of Helvetia. In the other direction, Hollybush School served a cluster of families about two miles northeast of the village, while a third school was attended by children who lived in the village center. The schools and neighborhoods created a focal point for otherwise isolated families. Children went to the same school, often stayed overnight with each other, and their parents worked together on school and farm projects. The clusters tended to become tight-knit groups often developing a group identity of their own. But while the terrain and school districts tended to divide the settlers, their religious services and other social events brought them together each week. People traveled long distances to band practice or to attend church in the central village location on Sundays.[20]

In addition to villagers and those nearby, two other clusters of Swiss and German immigrants were established at a greater distance from Helvetia on land sold by Lutz and Pickens. Several Swiss families settled high on Turkeybone Mountain about ten miles from Helvetia, while another group aggregated

Students at the Haslebacher School c. 1912. Haslebacher was one of three one-room schools that served the community for over fifty years. Aegerter photo.

just over the Randolph County line near present-day Holly River State Park in Webster County, some fifteen miles from Helvetia. These families were cut off from the village by several hours travel on foot or horse and found themselves extremely isolated with no stores or post offices nearby. As the most distant clusters, they participated least in Helvetia events and developed in many respects separate communities. By 1900, eight Swiss families lived on Turkeybone Mountain and seven in Webster County. It was also at Turkeybone that a group of fourteen German Catholic families settled, several of whom migrated together from Schenectady, New York. Together with the Swiss, they made Turkeybone the largest

Taken on a pleasant autumn day about 1905, this photo shows the visit of friends and relatives to the Bürki home on Turkeybone Mountain. Such Sunday visiting usually included the entire family. Aegerter photo.

cluster with 119 men, women, and children. As the town of Pickens on Right Fork of the Buckhannon became a booming lumber town in the 1890s, the two groups looked increasingly to this nearer town as an economic and service center. Social ties remained,

however, among all the clusters as visiting, courting, and church services brought many of them together on Sundays and other holidays. [21]

Thus, like most communities, Helvetia developed divisions of neighborhood and school districts appropriate to its needs. These, however, were not the result of social class, religion, or nationalistic differences. The clusters were not, for example, exclusively Swiss or German, Catholic or Protestant, or artisans or farmers. There was a high degree of integration across the settlement area. The patterns of settlement at Helvetia were instead closely related to agricultural needs and topography. Lutz's endeavors to plan a village that would attract tradesmen, the scarcity of farmable land, and the barriers to transportation and communication in the mountains worked together to create a geographically decentralized community with a strong village nucleus. [22]

The cooperative and associative ways of the immigrants made the clusters into supporting units and the larger community into an important social network. Helvetia, as such, was not defined by municipal or corporate boundaries, but by the origin of its members. Those who spoke German, who participated in community events, who attended church, or were active in various social organizations, were considered part of the community no matter how far-flung their homesteads. These social bonds, as well as the educational and vocational backgrounds of the immigrants made an enduring community possible. The settlers arrived with the skills and experience of adult craftsmen, coupled with the energy and stamina of a young population. As a whole, they possessed good health and the ability to cooperate, without which the settlement would have disintegrated. With ingenuity and hard work, they slowly built a new community based on a sense of cultural identity and on sound practices of ecology and agriculture.

Chapter 4

An Agricultural Way of Life

FARMING IS A KIND of wedding between man and nature, which in the case of Helvetia involved sturdy, capable people living on rugged, unwilling land. Nature's gifts of abundant wildlife, wild fruits, and forests, which first so impressed the settlers, were counterbalanced by the difficult work of clearing and the shortage of arable land. The settlers soon discovered disadvantages that even hard work and good farming practices could not overcome. The excellent farmland of the Midwest, or for that matter, much of Ohio and Pennsylvania, was scarce in central West Virginia. Particularly in the upland region where Helvetia lay, the slope of the mountains and their susceptibility to erosion made farming very difficult. The hills surrounding the village rose from narrow valleys at the steep ratio of about four to one. Only on the mountaintops were there small strips of more gently rolling land. In the soil classification system used by the U.S. Department of Agriculture, which rates agricultural land on a continuum from Class I (Excellent) to Class VIII (Very Poor), most land on the Upper Buckhannon watershed falls into Class VII. These lands are described as having "severe limitations that make them unsuitable for cultivation and that restrict their use largely to very limited grazing, woodland, or wildlife food and cover." Steep slopes, erosion, shallow soil, and stones are the land's primary characteristics. [1]

The ridges along the tops of the hills, however, comprised a small area somewhat more suited to agriculture, falling generally into Class III and/or IV, with slopes ranging from 10 to 20 percent. These narrow strips are well-drained, yet have the ability to retain water in the subsoils during dry periods.

A well-kept mountaintop farm typical of those at Helvetia. Land has been cleared along a gently rolling ridge. Barns and fences are well maintained and hay shocks have been placed in the meadows after a recent haying. n.d. Aegerter photo.

Their medium texture makes them easy to work and allows plant roots to penetrate without difficulty. The soils, however, are moderately to strongly acidic with low inherent fertility, making even the care of pastures a perpetual task. In short, the soil and terrain offered only the most basic essentials to the farmer and these in very limited amounts. [2]

Helvetia's climate, on the other hand, was more favorable. Between the years 1877 and 1929 the average temperature for January (the coldest month) was

A few homesteads were set in the narrow bottom lands as the one pictured here. This photo shows several features common to Helvetia farms, including the settlement cabin on the left, kept as an outbuilding after construction of the frame house, and a large garden plot, far right. The barn is nestled toward the back of the farm. n.d. Aegerter photo.

30.7°F and July (the warmest month) 68.4°F. The average annual temperature recorded for this fifty-two-year period was a warm 49°F. Although the average temperature for the months of harvest was far above freezing (50°F–60°F), the elevation of the area, which at Helvetia is 2,600 feet and reaches 3,700 feet above sea level at Turkeybone Mountain, made early frosts quite common. As a result, the growing season was a short 140–159 days a year. [3] Usually heavy rainfalls, however, helped to mitigate the short growing season.

Those who didn't have horses sometimes used oxen, or even cows trained as oxen, to pull farm machinery. Here, Noah Egleson and his son Edwin are pictured with their mower and white cow "Schimmel," c. 1890. Courtesy Mary Huber Marti.

During the same fifty-two-year period the average annual precipitation was 64.85 inches. This abundance of rain, often the largest recorded amounts in the state, helped to account for the lush forest and plant growth, but added to the constant threat of soil erosion on cleared land. [4]

The combination of these geographic features, along with the sheer isolation of Helvetia from economic centers, assured a strictly subsistence way of life in the three decades preceding 1900. During these years, the settlers worked to create a viable economy in which self-sufficient farming, hunting, and gathering were honed to great efficiency. Through sound methods, they slowly and meticulously developed each farmstead into a useful block of land capable of feeding their growing families. From 1869 until the mid-1950s, agriculture remained a vital way of life, providing a primary basis for self-sufficiency, cooperative work, and community integration.

When the land around Helvetia was first divided into farms, it was surveyed so that each farmer received a similar complement of land and resources. The property boundaries often formed saddles over the ridges, creating parcels with mountaintop land in the center and sloping land on one or both sides of it. Of these 100- to 200-acre farms, usually no more than one-half was cleared. The best land was used for planting crops and growing hay, while the steepest was used as a woodlot. Cattle were turned out to forage in the woods the entire summer, which was typical for the area, and resembled the practice of summer grazing in the Alps of Switzerland. Through the careful cultivation of the land, as well as hunting and gathering, the settlers were able to feed everyone in the settlement and accumulate small surpluses within a few years of their arrival. [5]

Records for the earliest years of agriculture in Helvetia are almost nonexistent except for a few cumulative statistics collected by Dr. Stucky in the mid-1870s. While perhaps slightly inflated, Stucky's figures show that by 1873 (and probably earlier), the settlers grew a variety of crops, which provided a nutritionally sound diet. That year their combined yields totaled 1,000 bushels of potatoes and 600 bushels of corn. Two years later (presumably with more land in production), they harvested 4,000 bushels of potatoes and 2,100 bushels of corn. The corn harvest would have been one-third greater, Stucky said, if not for an early September frost! The large potato yield, averaging from 100 to 150 bushels per acre, represented 10.5 bushels of potatoes for every man, woman, and child in the settlement. This exceeded potato yields in Randolph County for 1900, a period of more advanced agricultural methods than 1875. [6]

The settlers also cultivated several grains not commonly grown in their upland region. Wheat, buckwheat, and rye harvested in small amounts were ground at the local gristmill and made into nutritious breads and cakes. Wild honey and maple sugar were gathered from the forest as a source of both food and money. During the 1870s, the settlers established an informal cooperative to make and sell maple syrup, soon an important source of income for the community. [7]

Although a wide variety of crops was quite apparent in early Helvetia, livestock and farm animals were slow to arrive because of their relatively high cost. Initially, only a few farmers could

This photo of the Haslebacher farm on Hilltop shows a forebay bank barn, which was unusual at Helvetia. Most barns built by the Swiss German settlers were gable-end bank barns with no forebay. When this barn burned, it was replaced with a gable-end bank barn. c. 1910. Aegerter photo.

Alfred Teuscher rides home after a day of plowing in a distant field. Horses were later used extensively for transportation as well as farming. n.d. Courtesy Mary Huber Marti.

afford an animal for riding or plowing. In 1875, the entire settlement had only ten horses, fifteen oxen, and three mules, a situation that required farming with only the most basic hand tools. The same year just twenty sheep could be counted among the settlers, but almost every family had acquired that most important food source, a milk cow. Pork was the most popular domestic meat, with some families owning two or three hogs, while beef cattle were very few. [8]

The Hofer farm looking south, 1921. Aegerter photo.

What is important to note from these figures is that once the land was cleared for planting, Helvetians harvested excellent yields per acre compared to their neighbors, and that even in the earliest years, while working with the simplest tools, they adequately fed their young families. From these stark beginnings, the settlers moved into a more secure self-sufficiency. What allowed them to progress under such circumstances may be justifiably called the art of subsistence living. Art, in this sense, defined

Women were also expected to help in the fields, as indicated by this haying photo of Henrietta and Ernest Hofer. c. 1905. Photo by Gottlieb Hofer.

as "human ingenuity in adapting natural things to man's use"—art which had been practiced in the mountains of Switzerland and Germany for centuries. Its essential requirements were a studied knowledge of sound farming techniques and tools; the ability to learn quickly by observation and experience; the practice of craftsmanship in building and repairing farm implements; and a strong measure of frugality, hard work, cooperation, and patience. That a great number of Swiss and Germans who migrated to Helvetia possessed these qualities is evident both by what we know of their background and by the ways they lived and farmed.

The importance of crop rotation and the use of fertilizer and lime were well known in Switzerland and were practiced by the settlers of Helvetia. They did not adopt the prevalent attitude on the American frontier of using up the land, then simply clearing a new area. As in Switzerland, farmable land around Helvetia was scarce, and it was carefully treated and conserved. Manure was saved throughout the winter and spread over the fields in early spring. Before commercial lime was available, a number of farmers saved animal bones, pulverizing them in bone-crushers and scattering the remains on their gardens.[9] The need to collect manure, coupled with hay and grain storage, made barns an essential part of each farm. Although cattle were allowed to roam free in the summer, they were provided with warm underground shelter throughout the winter in the moderate-to-large bank barns that Helvetia farmers constructed. Agriculture as a science was very much part of their world, as many people experimented with different crops, seed varieties, and methods to discover what would work best in their new environment. Some of the farmers read extensively on these subjects, subscribing to *The American Agriculturalist* and other such journals. Having lived in the northern and western states, many were also familiar with the use of current farming machinery, and when affordable they put

these new horse-drawn tools into use. As a result, the mowing machine and rake, seeders, threshing machines, and plows of varying design were part of the landscape around Helvetia before they were common to other mountain farms.[10]

In addition to their keen interest in farming methods, Helvetians had the ability to build and repair many of the tools they used. Horses could be shod, wagons constructed, harnesses and singletrees made on the farm or that of a neighbor's—capabilities which conserved untold time, money, and machinery. One startling example is that of a homemade threshing machine, constructed by the Zumbach family, Swiss settlers who moved to Helvetia from Ohio. A very talented group, the family produced in the next generations a blacksmith, gunsmith, millwright, cabinetmaker, and several musicians, none of whom had formal training in these vocations. [11]

Putting such skills to work in everyday life, however, was the test of subsistence living. It required that the entire family work together as an economic unit, growing and gathering food to feed its members. Central to their art was a carefully cultivated garden, which after it had been plowed in the spring, become the almost exclusive province of the women and children. Many days were spent throughout the summer hoeing, watering, and finally harvesting the large variety of vegetables that were cultivated. To these were added wild fruits, the blackberries, strawberries, and service berries which thrived in the clearings where they were allowed to grow, as well as the abundant chestnuts and hickory nuts which were easily stored through the winter. The settlers wasted no time in planting domestic fruits and nuts too. Apple, pear, cherry, and plum trees were nursed with great care, as were walnuts and two or three varieties of grapes. The surplus harvest was stored in underground cellars beneath the farmhouses for use during the winter. Before canning became common practice, fruits, meats, and some vegetables were dried in a smokehouse and eaten as they were needed. [12]

Just as the cooperation of each family member was essential, so was that of the neighbors. From the first years when several families lived under one roof to later when there were barns to raise and hay to make, life in Helvetia included mutual support. The difficulties of pioneering were made easier by a strong sense of community, as seasonal work often became time for festivity and hospitality. Cornhusking, threshing, butchering, haymaking, and woodcutting were all eagerly anticipated events. The women fixed large meals for the crews, and everyone worked from daylight until dark to get the work done. In the evening, the families gathered for a dance or party and visited into the night. This yearly agricultural cycle fostered a sense of continuity with the rhythms of nature and reaffirmed important feelings of human support and caring. [13]

During such laborious and festive events the custom of serving wine was never ignored. Virtual-

Children and relatives helped dig potatoes in this shot of harvesting at the Herman Schneider farm. Made into a postcard, this photo was sent to relatives in Switzerland to show the family and harvest, c. 1920. Courtesy Alwin Schneider.

ly every household made wine, and it was treated as the everyday drink it was in Europe. No day was finished without a glass of wine, no visit to a neighbor complete without wine and cheese from the cellar. Several different wines were made from the various domestic and wild fruits, with grape, blackberry, and elderberry as the standard fare. As far as is known, no one in Helvetia ever attempted to produce wine commercially or even to age it for long periods of time. The desire was a pleasant table wine suitable for family, friends, and well-known visitors. [14]

The mutual support so important among the immigrants during these early years was enhanced by a feeling of equality; equality in the sense that in their new situation, their economic means and worldly possessions were roughly similar to each other. The first generation worked primarily at establishing complete and workable farms, and any savings went to this immense task. In a subsistence economy, artisans farmed the land and farmers worked to wright wheels and build cabinets. There was little, if any, opportunity to accumulate wealth. This economic relationship of Helvetia families is poignantly reflected in the property records for the year 1895. Of sixty-one families and individuals listed, their average taxable personal property (excluding land) was valued at a slim $88.87. The range was from $1.00 to $337.00, with the most conspicuous items being clocks, watches, and musical instruments, probably brought with them from Europe. [15] Thus, there was little room for social class distinctions or social mobility. After twenty-five years, Helvetia was not a rich community by material standards, although it was fertile with vocational ability and maintained a generous cultural life. Particularly in the early years of the settlement, but to a large extent throughout its history, Helvetia remained a virtually classless community of skilled farmers.

By the turn of the century, however, Helvetia's social and economic life began a fundamental change. The isolation of the community yielded to outsiders coming to harvest the surrounding virgin forests. Migrant timber workers and railroads began to infringe on an otherwise peaceful way of life. Jobs in industry suddenly became available, and farmers began to produce food for the lumber camps that were built in almost every hollow. These trends, taken up in depth in the following chapter, affected, but did not overwhelm, the community's agricultural way of life. Instead, they produced incentive to grow more and to engage in a market economy with those who needed food and services. During the years between 1900 and 1925, Helvetians increasingly looked to area lumber camps and hotels as a market for homegrown food, slowly becoming accustomed to growing cash crops and looking more toward the marketplace.

This change in orientation became most important after 1910 as the Agricultural Extension Service created new ways to market West Virginia's agricultural commodities. By establishing cooperatives to collect and sell the products of small farmers in larger quantities, new markets became available. When an agricultural extension agent visited Helvetia in 1917, urging the organization of a local farm cooperative and offering to help improve yields through scientific methods, he found local farmers very receptive. On November 9, 1917, they organized the Helvetia Farm Men's

A "woodcutting" at Helvetia—neighbors gathered to help cut firewood for the winter. Such cooperative efforts were common among Helvetia farmers, c. 1905. Aegerter photo.

Club, which met regularly the first Sunday of every month to plan and discuss numerous joint projects. Extension agents traveled from Elkins, the county seat, almost every month to meet with the club, bringing ideas and information for their consideration. They suggested the use of various types of fertilizer and lime, as well as good drainage practices, crop rotation procedures, and the reseeding of pastures with better varieties of alfalfa and clover. Periodically, they gave presentations on such topics as purebred livestock, insect control, and tuberculosis in cattle. They also arranged for the club to purchase bulk orders of feed, lime, fertilizer, salt, and plant seed. These were shipped via the Baltimore and Ohio Branchline at Pickens, and a club member designated as the purchasing agent arranged for their distribution to club members. [16]

In the club's strongest years of the 1920s and '30s, it had thirty to forty members (i.e., male heads of household), and found its leadership primarily from A. B. Cressler, John J. Betler, Herman Schneider, George Anderegg, and Arnold Metzener, who served as the officers of the club for over two decades. The group's primary source of income came from the 25¢ to 50¢ annual dues required from each member. Dues for families of deceased members were paid by the club, and such monies were spent for travel to various county and state meetings and for refreshments and music after local meetings. [17]

The farm club also developed several ways to ship produce cooperatively to outside markets via the B&O Railway. In 1926 they organized the Middlefork Livestock Shippers Association, with John J. Betler as president. This small, semi-independent body worked with Upshur County Livestock Shippers Association to sell cattle, sheep, and lambs to markets as far away as New York and Boston. As an example of their work, in 1928, the club sold a total of 660 lambs at 13.5¢ per pound, which grossed the farmers $8,528.08—an average of $172.00 per farmer. Although this was a very small income, together with other sales it helped produce cash needed to buy commercially made items. [18] The Helvetia-Pickens Wool Pool and the Helvetia Poultry Association were organized along similar lines to increase production and sales. The poultry business was particularly attractive to local farmers because it offered a weekly income. In the first year of the cooperative (1926), forty-two producers signed up, and two packing stations were designated. By 1928 the farmers were producing just under 500 dozen eggs a month for the market, at an average of 33.5¢ per dozen. The tiny, but consistent cash flow made all the difference in household economies which often just hoped to break even at the end of the year. [19]

One important venture that the club failed to develop, however, was the cooperative production and sale of cheese. A tasty cheese, similar to that made in Swiss alpine communities, had been made in Helvetia since the first cow arrived. As early as the 1880s Helvetians hoped to make the sale of cheese a lucrative business. John Teuscher and John Bürki, two Bernese Swiss, set up a small *Käserei* at the Teuscher farm in the village. They built a small milk house with cold running water to cool the milk, then brought it to the proper temperature in a large copper kettle placed over a wood fire. The men purchased surplus milk from the local farmers, churned the cream into butter, and molded the milk curd into large circular wheels of cheese. It was cured in the moist environment of Teuscher's cellar. There was limited sale for the product in the area because most farmers made their own, and the problems of shipping it were compounded by the lack of rail service. Consequently, the commercial aspect of the venture did not mature.[20]

The potential, of course, existed and when the railroad did come to nearby communities, farmers such as Christian Zumbach shipped cheese to Baltimore, Chicago and other cities. Zumbach had a mountaintop farm on which he maintained eight to ten dairy cows and produced from ten to twenty pounds of cheese daily. He and the other area farmers produced cheese for distant markets as a home industry until the railroad refused to ship such small quantities of farm produce. They continued to sell the product to timber workers and visitors, but the idea of a community cheese factory did not recur until the early 1930s. Then, at the suggestion of the Extension Service, the Farm Men's Club discussed the possibility over the course of a couple years, but never made it an important goal. The idea was allowed to die, probably due in part to the economic atmosphere of the Depression years and the wishes of some members to have it remain solely a family business in all aspects. In the long run, this was a critical omission on the part of the farmers, because it would have supplied the entire community with a locally owned business and economic mainstay. As a result, cheesemaking remained a family business that depended primarily on people who came to the farms or local stores to buy it.[21]

As a whole, however, the Farm Men's activities were effective and essential to maintaining a strong community in a changing economy. Their efforts were matched by an equally active Farm Women's Club, which in addition to keeping abreast of the latest food preservation techniques, supplied much of the labor and fundraising for special community events. After its founding in 1920, the club never disbanded, continuing to hold an annual Chicken Supper and other events to raise money for the Farm Clubs' joint undertaking of the annual Community Fair. This event, considered by extension leaders in 1929 as the most complete agricultural exhibit in the county, persists as an annual celebration to this day.[22]

With such institutions in place, Helvetia entered the Depression of the 1930s a well-organized and prepared community. In many ways, the economic crisis created a throwback to the earlier days of subsistence when, as children, the elder members of the community practiced the art of self-sufficient living. Life on these small farms had still not changed so much that the transition was a great one. According to Ella Betler, a young Helvetia woman who raised several children during the 1930s, "the Depression didn't bother us too much." She recalled that "we had a lot of crops," and as "far as clothes were concerned, we used our feed sacks and made our children's clothes, but to me it was happy days, because you pulled together and made everything reach and do . . . There was no money, but we never went cold or we never went hungry."[23] Some families were hit harder by the crisis than others, but Helvetians, by and large, did not suffer, due to a well-developed safety net of tillable farms and cooperative organizations. The hard times simply called on the community to do the things it knew best.

During the 1920s and '30s, the Extension Service worked hard to improve farm efficiency and community life all over West Virginia, and among extension workers, Helvetia was often considered an ideal small community. It was held up as a self-sufficient, cooperative unit, where new ideas were welcome and farmers were well organized. "No community in West Virginia has forged ahead more rapidly . . . than Helvetia," wrote a Randolph County Extension Agent in 1925, "all as a result of progressive spirit shown by its citizens, who are among the most thrifty and successful people in the county." Several years later, during the Depression, he suggested that, "If all the state would cooperate as well as these Swiss folks do who inhabit this community . . . we would have a state that was about perfect in all their community undertakings." [24] During this time, the Farm Men and Women succeeded in winning several community betterment awards for receiving high scores in areas such as health, schools, churches, businesses, and farms, while continually receiving the praise of people in the extension field. [25]

If one can speak of a "golden period" of agriculture or community spirit, the years between the two world wars were certainly that for Helvetia. The rugged, small mountain farms were brought to their fullest potential under the cooperative efforts of the local farmers, encouraged by county extension specialists. More produce was raised, and more sold, than at any other time in the community's history. The farmers were proud of their accomplishments and earned a reputation as hardworking and successful people. The photos taken of the community during this time, and as early as 1900, show carefully groomed fields, and well-built houses, fences, and barns pleasingly located on the mountainous landscape. The people were well dressed, sturdy, and showed a sense of humor and dignity amid their surroundings. Clearly, in spite of the geographical disadvantages, the immigrants managed to create a prosperous life.

Throughout the early years of subsistence agriculture and up to World War II, Helvetians depended upon their ingenuity to shape and adapt the natural environment. Numerous craftsmen and innovative farmers contributed to the community's evolution, and those who were hardworking, frugal, and patient gained returns both in income and personal satisfaction. Extended families worked together as economic units and the entire community was a system of support and help. Helvetians had the security and freedom of self-reliance because they controlled the means to sustain their own way of life. After the Second World War, however, the efficiency of western farming caught up with Helvetia, as it did with most small farms in America. Unable to hold many of its young people who left for jobs in the cities, the community's population shrank. Farming was left for those who could combine its money-saving aspects with jobs in lumber, coal mining, school teaching, and other industrial and service occupations. In the 1950s, a number of people bought tractors and began converting to modern hayrakes, balers, and other laborsaving equipment, but by 1960, agriculture as a distinct way of life in Helvetia had run its course—its central place in community affairs had ended. What remained was a vivid, often romanticized, memory of those years when Helvetia was a community of farmers held together by a common heritage and adventure—a place where life revolved around the rhythms of nature and people's relationships were based on the work they did both individually and cooperatively. [26]

Chapter 5

Forces of Change

When Helvetia's settlers arrived in the 1870s West Virginia had 10 million acres of virgin forest. By 1920 it was gone. In the intervening years the state's economy was transformed and controlled by the leaders of extractive industries such as wood, coal, oil, and gas, who sent the resources and most of the profit out of West Virginia. The ensuing cycles of boom and bust produced by such businesses invariably left the small mountain towns reeling from one economic surge to another. Those communities that, like Helvetia, were on the fringes of the heaviest industrialization were spared the worst environmental and social violence of the period, but were greatly affected by the general economic trends.[1]

It was not an accident when, in 1892, a branch line of the B&O Railroad was built from Alexander in Upshur County to near the small village of Florence on the Right Fork of the Buckhannon River, just five miles from Helvetia. James Pickens, the area land developer and agent who succeeded Charles Lutz, used his connections to see that the rail line was built near his own holdings in the area. He soon parlayed the development into a small fortune as a new town by his name quickly began to boom. Within three years, the Pickens Lumber Company was employing 100 men who produced 35,000 board feet of lumber a day. In this short time, five hotels, four general stores, two barbershops, a drugstore, jewelry store, saloon, church, and furniture store were built in Pickens. In addition to carrying lumber, the rail line also provided passenger service to Buckhannon and beyond. The growth it spawned was unprecedented in this isolated section of Randolph County.[2]

No steel rail was to enter Helvetia for two more decades, but the community was soon linked to the new industry by other means. By 1900 a wooden tramway ran through Helvetia and along the stream to Newlonton (six and a half miles away) where logs could be sold or transferred. In several adjacent valleys and over mountains these wooden tramways were constructed to bring logs to meet the steel rails and coal locomotives. Building tramways through the mountains was a slow and labor-intensive process, often requiring elevation over streams and other obstacles. The system was, nonetheless, very useful because it provided access to areas where it was not feasible to build more expensive steel railroads, and it avoided the problems of hauling on muddy, unimproved dirt roads. Due to the tramway and the developments at Pickens, Helvetians became involved in the lumber industry almost as soon as the market developed on the upper Buckhannon River.[3]

The greatest impact of the industry did not hit the community, however, until 1915, when the Buckhannon Chemical Company laid a narrow gauge railway from Chemical, in Upshur County, to Helvetia to supply its chemical plant with additional hardwoods. Established in 1908, the company manufactured wood alcohol, acetate of lime, and charcoal from the native beech, maple, and cherry forests. By 1916 its hardy appetite was consuming 18,000 cords of wood a year, quickly turning the area forests into fields of stubble and culls. The new line became known as the Chemical-Hel-

View of an elevated tramway running through the mountains near Helvetia. Here the photographer is documenting a derailed tramcar on a winter day in c. 1910. Aegerter photo.

vetia Railroad, and in the following year, the main tracks and several branches were extended beyond Helvetia along most of the tiny tributaries in the area. This operation, as well as others in the area, supplied many Helvetians with what they called "public work" and gave the farmers sale for all of their hardwood timber. Many worked at cutting

Lumber camps such as the one glimpsed in this photo were built adjacent to the railroad that cut a narrow path through the forest. Shown at left are a few bunkhouses and a young family probably in charge of the camp, c. 1910. Aegerter photo.

their own trees, while others found jobs at the mills or in the lumber camps established for the many migrant timber cutters.[4]

During this time, the community became host to a variety of migrant workers, typically recent immigrants from Austria-Hungary and Italy. Some came with families, but the majority were young, single men who had gained a reputation in other parts of the county for drinking and fighting. This behavior, of course, was not unknown in Helvetia, but some felt the workers threatened the social and moral fabric of the community. One clergyman viewed the "majority" of the workers as " . . . a rough class, the scum from elsewhere, worldly minded, resorting to gambling and other ill practices." "The spiritual life of the church people," he wrote in a church history, "was much influenced and ill effected to materialism, desecration of the Sabbath, profanity and drinking."[5]

While such behavior might have caused some people concern, many were also sympathetic to the workers' situation. The camps where they lived consisted of a few roughly built frame buildings, which served as bunkhouse, kitchen-dining room, horse barn, and blacksmith shops. The quarters were cramped, and the absence of bathing facilities contributed to the prevalence of scabies, a tormenting skin disease caused by tiny parasites. The problem was so common in the lumber camps that it was simply called "camp itch."[6]

Notwithstanding these conditions, many young Helvetia men got their first taste of the new industrial system in the lumber camps. Some worked year-round, but jobs were so plentiful that the men would often work for short periods of time in the winter, then quit to plant crops for a change of pace. Later, they might get a job with a neighboring operation or even the same one. Their experience with work animals and tools made them readily employable as log skidders and timber cutters. [7]

If the timber industry had some hazards, it also brought numerous benefits. For the first time local farmers had an easily accessible market for their agricultural produce. Even though working at the mill or in the woods took some fathers and sons away from the farm, the small mountain homesteads began to grow extra produce for sale to the lumber camps and local hotels. Fresh vegetables, fruits, bread, butter, cheese, and other items went out to feed the increasing numbers of local timber workers, while farm families received cash in return.[8]

The timber boom also provided an opportunity for a few local entrepreneurs. Although most lumber operations around Helvetia were owned by outside companies, local men such as Balthasar Merkli set up mills which supplied lumber and building materials to the community. These mills, coupled with timber sales, income from agricultural products, wages, and services, provided a greater infusion of cash into Helvetia's economy than ever before. Suddenly, work animals and farm equipment that before had been too expensive became affordable, as did gasoline powered engines and home Delco units. The latter, a system of rechargeable batteries capable of producing enough electricity to light a house or keep baby chicks warm on a cold winter night, was used by some families before commercial electricity was available. An increased cash income also made it possible for children in large families to have more than one pair of shoes and for parents to purchase small, but special, mail-order items for Christmas. In important ways, the new economy raised the standard of living in the community and allowed "frills," which before had been out of the question. Although it remained difficult to transport goods in and out of the area, Helvetia's economic isolation ended as it became more a part of the regional economy.[9]

Leisure activities also began to reflect outside influences. On Sundays, the only day off, the railroad supplied special trains for the many town baseball teams organized along the rail lines. The second-generation Helvetia men and boys enjoyed the popular American sport. A level section of the Metzener family's cow pasture was measured off for a baseball diamond, and became the scene of many Sunday afternoon gatherings, as families and girlfriends turned out to support the team.[10]

More abrupt shifts toward an American outlook also occurred during this time. World War I cast a gloomy shadow over the community's newfound prosperity. The conflict took on special meaning for the families of German descent who still had families in Germany, as it did for the Swiss who were often thought to be German. Although Helvetia sent many of its young men into U.S. service, it, like other Germanic communities in the United States, came under suspicion because its people were Germanic or simply because they spoke a German dialect. In the spring of 1917 a number of West Virginia newspapers carried the story that "a battle between Americans and Germans in the remote part of Randolph County" was being waged, "following the hosting of the German flag over the village of Helvetia, a German settlement."

The sensational report said that patriotic Americans in the neighborhood tore down the "Teutonic colors," and a fight ensued. With "serious danger of bloodshed" still present, the sheriff was being dispatched to the scene.[11] The following month a dubious disclaimer from Helvetia appeared in the *Elkins Inter-Mountain* suggesting the report had been invented and inviting anyone who would to visit the community and judge for themselves.

> Many farmers are doing additional planting this year, [for the war effort]. Rev. B. H. Holtkamp cleaned up the bottom field of the cemetery and planted it in potatoes and corn. You understand we are patriotic, and on the 30th, we will have our flag raising at HELVETIA, W. VA. We want to be patriotic … Call on us and be convinced that we are the best PATRIOTS of West Virginia.[12]

This isolated and exaggerated incident obviously embarrassed the community, which managed successfully thereafter to maintain a patriotic reputation. It illustrates, however, the great pressure placed on Germanic communities during World War I to prove their allegiance to the United States. Such experiences, coupled with a greater awareness of the outside world fostered by the timber industry, began to undermine the strong ethnic identity of the community. For the first time, the importance of being an "American" began to overshadow the old identification with Switzerland or Germany.

The Helvetia Baseball Team (HBBT) as it appeared in about 1910. Left to right, Ben Fahrner, Arnold Metzener, Frank Wuerzer, Emmanuel Gimmel, John Marti, Walter Aegerter, Simon Gimmel, Alfred Koerner, unidentified. Aegerter photo.

Throughout World War I and into the 1920s, the timber boom continued to stimulate the economy and to cause serious environmental damage to the local area. The hills were virtually denuded by the clear-cutting practices of the chemical wood industry.

Brush fires and erosion became constant problems in the heavily cut over areas, and the streams were muddied to an extent unknown before. This marked the decline of native brook trout, which required relatively silt-free water for hatching its eggs. However, as the briars and undergrowth began to cover the forest floor, abundant habitat was created for small game, and with the enforcement of game laws over the entire state, the white-tailed deer began a comeback after severe overhunting.[13]

When the prime timber harvest was over in the mid-1920s, the Buckhannon Chemical Company took a few last trains to Helvetia in order to pick up their tracks. In each hollow the steel rails were wrenched from their timbers, loaded onto a freight car, and hauled away. The railroad disappeared like a mysterious beast that clambered through the mountains picking up its footprints as it went. The boom was over. With it went the jobs, both in industry and local businesses, that depended on it. The migrant workers moved on to the next area of operation, with the exception of a few families who put down roots in the community. Nearby, only the Pickens Branch Line remained. The lumber industry did not totally die in Pickens, although the town suffered greatly under the ensuing slowdown.[14]

Helvetia, however, had not sprung to life because of the timber industry, and it did not vanish in its wake like many boomtowns along the rail lines. Much to the credit of the women who stayed home to run the farms, agricultural productivity and profits increased during the boom years. Through the use of better tools, machinery, and rail transportation, the local farms strengthened their capacity to grow crops and found it profitable for the first time to raise livestock for market. As a result of these investments

at home, the community found itself better prepared for the hard times of the 1930s than communities that had grown dependent on industry.[15]

The lumber companies on the other hand had invested only what was necessary to cut and extract the virgin timber. They left behind few, if any, civic improvements as a result of tax dollars or direct community support. Generally, the quality of the schools, roads, and medical care did not improve with the harvest of timber wealth. In these areas there was little progress, leaving those without jobs or savings disillusioned with the promises of future prosperity. The most significant impact of the industry was, however, more subtle, for it was the harbinger of changes in a lifestyle much more basic to the community. It introduced to the next generation of Helvetians a developed cash economy and a taste for those things that only the local store or mail-order catalog could supply. Money, more than ever before, became important and necessary to carry on everyday affairs. Although the farm remained temporarily intact, once men were used to working for wages and area economies began to change, there was no turning back the clock. Perhaps people had been influenced by materialism, as the Helvetia pastor had earlier suggested, or perhaps more simply, the community had entered the twentieth century.[16]

The new century also brought technological changes that had the power to alter community life. Helvetia shared the nation's excitement over the automobile, radio, telephone, and other important innovations. By 1909 periodicals reaching the community advertised Western Electric's "Rural Telephone," which offered to solve the relative isolation of rural living. "The phone," one ad suggested, "will bring you and your family into closer touch with your neighbors, the general store, the broker, the post office, the family doctor, and the entire outside world. It does away with the isolation of farm life and keeps the boy on the farm." These were promises few could resist, and under the leadership of Helvetia pastor Benjamin Holtkamp, the community acquired telephone service in 1912, using the wooden magneto phones of the era. The service was initially provided through the People's Telephone Company of Jane Lew, but when the company went bankrupt in 1923, threatening the community with loss of service, the Helvetia Telephone Company was quickly incorporated. Stockholders paid $10.00 a share which helped cover a $2,300 debt of the bankrupt firm. Initially, Helvetia's forty customers paid only $1.00 a month for service, and to make sure everyone was in closer touch with the general store, post office, pastor, and community hall, these locations were given free service. Maintained and supported by the community, its charges never exceeding $2.00 per month, the system survived until 1966 when it was finally replaced by a modern Bell system.[17]

In the end, the telephone did not keep the boy on the farm, but it did revolutionize the way people interacted. It allowed last minute setting or changing of meeting dates. It saved time in efforts to organize a quilting or woodcutting and brought neighbors running at a second's notice in case of an emergency. The telephone was one innovation the community discovered it could not do without.

Helvetia, in fact, was without a hard surfaced road far longer than without telephones. In the 1920s and '30s the county graded and improved roads between Pickens, Helvetia, and Mill Creek (twenty-two miles away), but it was not until 1948 that a paved road was made from the two communities to Mill Creek. This, with the increased use of the automobile, finally made it convenient to travel to the county seat of government (Elkins), over forty miles away, and return the same day! The corollary, however, was that two years later passenger service to Buckhannon was discontinued on the Pickens Branch Line, due, at least in part, to a lack of use.[18]

Perhaps the one development which changed people's everyday lives most was electricity. Arriving about 1939, commercial electricity was so long in coming to the area that even as the lines were being installed, locals speculated about how long it would take the current to travel from the switching station once it was turned on. With it came electric lights, washing machines, ranges, water-pumps, and many other appliances that transformed life on the local farms. The "magic" of electricity was rediscovered in the isolated mountain region as oil lamps and candles were put aside for only occasional use. Now, the flip of a switch would illuminate an entire room. In the kitchens, the wood cookstove remained a favorite,

The switchboard for the locally operated telephone company that served the community from 1912 to 1966. One of the battery powered phone sets used in area homes is shown in the upper right of the photo. No calls were forwarded in the early evening while the operator was out to milk the cows! Photo by David H. Sutton.

but it eventually gave way to the electric range, saving a great deal of time and energy in getting wood and building fires for cooking. Large gatherings to cut wood became much less necessary. The washboard was also retired in many homes in favor of a washing machine with an electric motor. Such items were expensive, of course, and came slowly into the community, but their power to make work easier and to free

time for leisure or outside work continued to make them attractive.[19]

Electricity also brought the radio to Helvetia just in time to hear the broadcasts about Pearl Harbor and the subsequent reports of America's involvement in a second world war. The events penetrated every home as young men and women went out to help the war effort. They left to serve in the armed forces, the Red Cross, and later to northern factories to find jobs in the war industries. A nationwide migration began to urban industrial centers, and Helvetia was no exception to the trend or its effects on rural areas. The quest for employment took from the community much of its youth and potential for further growth. Those who remained were predominantly older people, who continued to live on the farms and receive the much-anticipated letters and visits from children in far-off cities such as Cleveland, Columbus, or Philadelphia.[20]

The one economic opportunity which allowed some younger people to stay, or to return, was the opening of several coal mines near the community. Although the coal industry began in other parts of West Virginia on the heels of the lumber boom, it did not reach Helvetia until the early 1940s. Generally, the local coal seams were quite thin and often irregular, making mining at best a speculative venture. However, with the development of large machinery to surface mine relatively shallow seams and an abundance of small adventuresome operators, the nearby town of Pickens, with its railroad, again became the site of industrial development. After

World War II, coal mining increasingly dominated the local economy, as it had in most areas of the state for many years. By the early 1960s it had cemented the changes introduced by the timber boom some fifty years earlier.[21]

In the course of this time, Helvetia was transformed from an agricultural community to an outpost for extractive industries. The introduction of such technologies as the telephone, commercial electricity, and the automobile revolutionized life in the mountains during the 1920s and '30s. The influences of two world wars against Germany and the distance of yet another generation from the old homeland helped to erode the sense of ethnic identity that had once prevailed. But the fundamental change was an economic one. During the earliest years of its life, Helvetia had developed the supportive social and economic patterns that were necessary for a life of subsistence agriculture. After the turn of the century, the community created a healthy interaction between the agricultural sector and a developing timber industry, which benefited both the farmers and timbermen.

However, as farming became less viable after World War II, it was replaced almost entirely by an industrial economy. Helvetia moved from being a community of farmers who lived by the yearly agricultural calendar to a community that followed the five-day workweek and whose inhabitants received wages for their labors. This was the most fundamental change because it removed the means of production from the community and placed it in the hands of outside interests. As more and more people began to work in industry or moved away to find jobs, Helvetians could no longer fall back on a safety net of carefully woven economic and social relationships as they had during the Depression. Nor could they easily reactivate the arts of self-sufficiency amid a cash economy. As a result, they increasingly faced the choice of seeking a way of life dependent on a volatile and often fragile coal industry or migrating from the home their immigrant ancestors had chosen. After the war, the latter choice was more common, and Helvetia became a tiny community with a few young wage earners and a large proportion of retired senior citizens.

Chapter 6

Continuity and Change: Helvetia's Social and Cultural Life

DESPITE THE MANY CHANGES and transitions through the years, Helvetia remained, for the most part, a small, cohesive community. Side by side with the forces of change were strong elements of continuity—elements which both bound people together and sought to interpret and use change to fit the needs of the community. These elements, partly tradition, partly the creative response to a new and changing way of life, were fostered by the social institutions the settlers established. The family, church, school, and cultural organizations structured community life, giving it meaning and direction amid social and economic change. These institutions reflect not only how the community chose to organize itself, but how its institutions met various community needs, and how changing needs over time spurred the process of acculturation and Americanization.

Helvetia's clubs and associations played important roles in organizing community life and transmitting tradition. The German Reformed Church, together with family and school, helped maintain the use of the German language and foster a feeling of connectedness to the mother country. Together these institutions helped meet community needs for a sense of continuity and cohesiveness during the many adjustments made by the immigrants and their children to a foreign environment.

The formation of societies and associations for athletics, hunting, or playing cards is well known in the United States, but it is even more common in Europe. There, associations have played a central part in community life for several centuries. The Swiss and Germans were particularly fond of organizing people to ski, hunt, hike, play music, and take part in a wide variety of activities. The Swiss are so prone to affiliation that they joke that wherever there are at least two Swiss, they will form an association or club.

This observation is reinforced by the fact that where Swiss and German communities were founded in the United States there was usually a predictable roster of associations established by the immigrants. These typically included a *Blechmusikgesellchaft* or brass band, a *Gesangverein* or choral society, a *Krankenunterstützungsverein*, or association for the mutual assistance of the sick, and often a benevolent society for economic assistance to the needy. In centers with a large German population such as New York, Cincinnati, or Milwaukee, these were often accompanied by a German press, as well as athletic, rifle, and other clubs. [1] In America, moreover, these organizations took on an added significance. They functioned not only to carry out their expressed purpose, but to perpetuate the community life and customs of the homeland among their fellow immigrants. In Helvetia, they also became the primary basis for conscious community organization.

In view of the central role which was played by clubs both in the United States and abroad, it is not surprising that the initial founding of Helvetia was carried out by a mutual aid society, the *Grütliverein* in Brooklyn, New York. In addition to providing a sense of security in the urban environment, the *Verein* acted as a springboard for those members who wished to migrate into the countryside. It sponsored

the expedition that investigated the West Virginia land, and although no record of it exists, may have offered economic support to the first families until they were established. The clubs were capable of filling a wide variety of needs, both economic and social, and it was according to pattern that a *Grütliverein* was in turn founded in early Helvetia, where the need for mutual assistance was often acute. [2]

In 1881, the *Verein* at Helvetia consisted of twelve male members who organized themselves on a democratic model, with Johannes Hofer (from Canton Bern) as president, Dr. Christian F. Stucky (Bern), as secretary, and Kasper Huber (Zürich), as treasurer. As a mutual aid society, they helped members who were ill during planting or harvesting times or behind in their work. If a member died, he was assured that his family would be taken care of, either by club members or through an insurance plan that was offered by the national affiliate, the North American Grütli Alliance. The club provided Helvetia firm contacts with Swiss in the outside world as well as mutual support from within. [3]

A second, equally important function of the *Verein* was to perpetuate a sense of continuity with the homeland. Members met each Sunday afternoon to discuss business, socialize, and to sing their favorite Swiss songs. These twelve disciples were among the first group to begin shaping cultural life along the typical lines of Swiss and German settlements. Exactly how long the *Grütliverein* continued

The Helvetia *Grütliverein* as it sat for a formal photograph about 1890. Left to right, front row: Mathias Suesli, Gottlieb Betler, Fredrich Wälchli, George Stadler; second row: Karl Dubach, John Wuerzer, Balthazar Merkli, Fredrich Haslebacher, Kasper Metzener; third row: Mr. Philomen (?), Kasper Huber, David Künzler. Photographer unknown.

actively is unknown, but around the turn of the century, as Helvetians became well established and developed the broad community support of friends, neighbors, and relatives, the guarded, institutionalized support of the *Verein* faded. The family clusters, as well as the larger community, began to fill the need for mutual support and caring, while a popular brass band supplied a rich tradition of music and song for the community. [4]

The band was organized formally in 1875 under the leadership of German watchmaker, Hermann Schloo. It quickly became an integral part of most social gatherings in the community, playing waltzes, polkas, schottisches, and marches from Europe

Helvetia Star Band, in uniform, as it appeared on postcard photos, c. 1912. The band played both European and American march and dance tunes, as well as hymns and dirges for funerals. Aegerter photo.

and later from the States. Like the *Grütliverein*, its membership was customarily male, but women often attended band practices to dance with each other or sing the songs of their childhood. The band supplied music for dancing and singing at all major community celebrations—including New Year's, *Fastnacht*—a pre-Lenten celebration, the Fourth of July, Sunday School picnics, the Community Fair, and other events. The community's musical traditions were among the most celebrated connections to the homeland and the most enjoyed recreation in early Helvetia. [5]

Helvetia Star Band, out of
uniform, as it appeared on
postcard photos, c. 1912.
Aegerter photo.

The popularity of dancing in turn, gave rise to the need for good dance halls. Helvetians quickly went from dancing under a local sawmill shed, to a small, but adequate frame building built for the purpose. This served until about 1901, when an elaborate dance hall was built across from the Daetwyler home in the center of the village. This second, beautifully designed hall, with native chestnut, tongue and groove wainscoting, and a

high, elevated bandstand, was built partially as a result of a split in the band. Disagreements between two members eventually led to a division of loyalties between musicians who lived in the village and those who lived in the Hilltop area. The Hilltop group retained the first, small dance hall, while the village group built the new building, naming it the Helvetia Star Band Hall after their organization. Although the band remained divided, tempers eventually cooled,

The Helvetia Brass Band at
the Pickens Cemetery, c. 1925.
Photographer unknown.

and music and dancing continued to be important community activities. [6]

The new dance hall became the scene for an increasing number of social events often attended by lumber and sawmill workers from nearby locations. Here, the Swiss and German music traditions met the fiddle tunes and square dances common to the Appalachian region. The "outsiders" were particularly fond of square dancing, and Helvetians were initially quite accommodating until the new dances began to take up increasingly long portions of the evening. At this, a rule was established governing

Together with brass music, the Swiss and Germans cultivated a tradition of string music accented by the familiar violin, but also influenced by Appalachian fiddle styles, banjo tunes, and other regional music. This gathering is at the Aegerter home, c. 1915. Aegerter photo.

the length of square dances, after which three couple dances (i.e., waltzes, polkas, etc.) were to be played before another square dance could begin. This compromise established a pattern that allowed both traditions to survive and which is evident at Helvetia dances up to the present.[7]

In spite of these trends to accommodate both traditions and the cliquish affairs of the band, brass music remained a part of community life until almost World War II. The bands actually provided a mechanism for integrating local traditions into the community without losing sight of their own musical heritage. They continued to fill the tremendous need of an isolated, rural community for family recreation and fun, while providing the leadership and manpower to sponsor community-wide events. The music they played continued to have a European theme that ran through all the events for which they performed.

The split in the band, however, impaired its ability to remain at the center of community leadership. As the important function of agricultural organizations became more apparent, the farm clubs became the leading associations in the community. Both the Farm Men's and Farm Women's Clubs played important roles in Helvetia's economy and social life throughout the 1920s, '30s, and '40s. They enjoyed very wide community support and were able to sponsor a variety of new events around which community life became focused. When their undertaking of a Community Fair outgrew the Star Band Hall, they built a new and larger hall (1939), with a space for exhibits downstairs and a large dance floor upstairs. In order to raise money to pay fair premiums, the Farm Women instituted an annual chicken supper. The event was conveniently scheduled in August, so that friends and relatives who had left the community could come back to visit for the occasion.[8]

In the 1940s, the Farm Men and Women also began the extremely popular Ramp Supper as a source of income for community projects. The ramp, a pungent leek which grows in most parts of the Appalachian range, was a favorite springtime food for central West Virginians when the settlers arrived. Helvetians, too, ate them for many years in the privacy of their own homes, but when a consumer taste for the wild plant arose, they organized an annual ramp dinner. Each year on the last weekend in April, it became common to serve from 800 to 1,000 guests at the community hall, many of whom had driven hours to share in a feast whose odor would not leave their breaths for at least three days![9]

Thus, as new economic and organizational needs arose in the community, new clubs were established to carry out the function. When the new community hall was completed, the Hall Association was formed to care for the property and oversee events there. The decision to hold the Community Fair brought a joint Fair Association committee together, and the desire to prepare young people for farming led to the establishment of 4-H clubs. In later years, as the community began to consciously preserve its heritage, clubs appropriate to the task were organized. The Helvetia Folk Dancers, Alpine Rose Garden Club, Helvetia Restoration and Development Association, and the Historical Society of Helvetia were founded chiefly for this purpose.

Throughout the community's history, the mechanism of the club was the key to community organization as well as social life. The town never incorporated under local statutes, nor did it adopt a system of town government based on European or American political models. The political and

A few members of the Helvetia Farm Men's and Farm Women's Club, c. 1950. Left to right, Rudolph Zumbach, Arnold Betler, Mary Zickefoose, Ella Betler, Arnold Metzener, Dale Daetwyler. Courtesy Mary Zickefoose.

social needs of the community were met by the clubs, which either took on the task or established a new group to do the job. It was a broadly democratic approach that offered a role for everyone who wished to participate, although the early clubs had very restricted roles for women. These various groups operated essentially like committees, which reported informally to each other, but never to a higher body. The sharing of responsibilities and the lack of a centrally elected administration assured, in the eyes of the community members, that

no one person or group collected too much power. As long as this remained the case, things ran relatively smoothly and community affairs were politically balanced.

Such a form of organization arose primarily because the Swiss and German cultural clubs met a situation that demanded a broader range of responsibilities than usual. In a very loosely organized settlement, the clubs provided an easy and familiar way to structure community life, as well as filling the needs for security, entertainment, and cooperation. As the need for leadership and direction became acute amid the chaos caused by Charles Lutz's endeavors, the clubs took on functions that were not normally in their realms. The *Grütliverein* not only assisted the sick, but functioned as a meeting of community leaders who wrote many letters protesting Lutz's business and immigration practices. The band not only supplied music and entertainment, its gathering brought together a wide cross-section of people who discussed current community projects and helped develop a consensus on the issues of the day. As clubs of American origin, such as the Farm Clubs, were established, the informal role of leadership passed on to them. Together they sponsored the major community events and set the tone and direction for social and cultural life in Helvetia. As carriers of tradition, they celebrated and reinforced the common heritage of their members. Yet, as community needs changed, they responded with the flexibility and continuity needed for healthy adjustment.

While clubs and associations helped sustain a sense of continuity in the secular world, the church was central to religious continuity. It fostered a familiar community of faith that reinforced the shared values, beliefs, and traditions of its members. At Helvetia, it institutionalized not only the ecclesiastical traditions of the German Reformed Church, but also the use of the German language in worship and church education. The church, for much of its history, was a key institution for the maintenance of the German language. This made

the later transition to the use of English a problematic one—a transition that can only be fully understood in the context of the church's establishment in the community.

The Reformed tradition, in which most of the immigrants had grown up, was by 1850 a tightly woven web of doctrine and practice. Since the Reformation it had evolved through many stages, setting aside and adopting several written confessions. Its doctrinal emphasis varied between Switzerland and Germany, and sometimes from one town to another. Its fundamental beliefs, however, were characterized by the Heidelberg Catechism. Its church life was often doctrinaire, rigorously disciplined, and concerned with details of church government.[10]

It is no surprise then, that the Helvetia settlers had a very firm idea of what was necessary to church life. A trained minister was essential, along with a body of elders, deacons, and trustees. The erection of a proper sanctuary for worship was also high on the priority list. From the increasing flow of settlers in 1873, the community found its first minister, the Rev. Andrew Kern. That fall, on September 7, 1873, a group of some fifty charter members organized a congregation under the name The German Evangelical Reformed Church at Helvetia, Randolph County, West Virginia. This was possible only after the hammering out of a detailed constitution and its endorsement by all the men in the group. From the membership, the group elected Johannes Anderegg and Christian Wenger as elders; Johannes Teuscher and Gustav Sennhauser as deacons; and Gottlieb Fahrner, Jakob Karlen Sr., and Dr. Christian F. Stucky as trustees. A log house owned by Wenger was temporarily rented for $2.00 a month for church services, catechismal instruction, and singing practice until a sanctuary could be built.[11]

On April 6, 1874, a special meeting of the officers decided to build a church fifty feet long, twenty-six feet wide, and eighteen feet high. The congregation was asked to contribute the necessary money, lumber, and labor for its construction, but capital was so scarce that there was no immediate success. The following year Rev. Kern resigned, leaving the task of the new sanctuary uncompleted. Little progress was made until 1880, when the settlement found an energetic clergyman named Franz Münzner to lead the building effort. Under his and the church committee's direction, the project moved ahead quickly. A centrally located town lot was donated by Nikolas Kaderly, a merchant from New Philadelphia, Ohio, who had invested in several Helvetia lots. Local sawmills gave 3,000 board feet of rough lumber, and thirty-four members of the congregation pledged a total of 110 days of labor. With new optimism the cornerstone of the church was laid the 11th of April 1880.[12]

A lack of money, however, still delayed the project. The costs of finishing the lumber, together with other building materials, quickly depleted the sanctuary fund. Rev. Münzner was asked to do a canvas of Reformed churches in northern West Virginia and southern Ohio in an effort to collect donations for the project. Although against the idea of what he later called "begging," he traveled throughout the region talking with and receiving donations from 225 individuals and groups. The long list of donors included wealthy landowners, such as Jonathan M. Bennett and Gidean D. Camden, who each gave a tiny sum of $1.00 toward the church. When the receipts were totaled, they came to $169.00. Still short of the necessary funds, the building committee stacked the lumber and waited for better times. The following spring of 1881, Rev. Münzner resigned.[13]

His canvas, however, had alerted the Reformed churches in Wheeling, West Virginia, and in southern Ohio to the needs of the Helvetia congregation. In the spring of 1882, the St. John's Classis, a regional division of the Central Synod of the Reformed Church in the United States, sent the Rev. Daniel Schroth to Helvetia as a mission worker. Schroth immediately reorganized the congregation under a new constitution with the title The German Evangelical Reformed Zions Church and brought it under the jurisdiction of the St. John's Classis. Charged by these positive events, the congregation added money to the building fund from local donations and possibly from the classis itself. During the summer of 1882 the sanctuary was completed, and on November 12, the members gathered inside for the first time to dedicate the building to God.[14]

In less than a year after its dedication the church was fully equipped and paid for. The cost was a total of $884.00 in cash, plus the cost of one-half the rough lumber and about 100 days of free labor. With this great obstacle overcome, the church grew rapidly, reaching a membership of 124 by 1889. The first manse was also built in the 1880s, and congregations were organized among the Swiss and Germans on Turkeybone Mountain and in Webster County. [15]

The congregation's relationship to the St. John's *Classis* remained a vital link for many years. The classis viewed the church in the wilderness as its *Sorgenkind* or literally, its child to care for, supplying it with ministers who were trained in the German church and spoke its language. Worship services were held entirely in German, German hymns were played and sung, and publications were purchased through the Reformed Publishing House in Cleveland, Ohio. Over the next fifty years the settlers and their children enjoyed and maintained religious services similar to the ones they had known in Europe. [16]

The church functioned, along with the family unit, to maintain the use of German language in the community. The first generation of Helvetians grew up in a decidedly Swiss German atmosphere. Their first language was German or Swiss German, their parents continued to speak dialect at home and when visiting friends and neighbors. In the church, it was considered essential that the children study the catechism in German, as well as learn to write

The Helvetia German Reformed Church as it appeared around 1900. Photographer unknown.

Easter Greetings. of Mont Zion Helveti from Susie Sto...

the language. Special summer classes, taught by the minister, were held at the church for this purpose each year. [17] Children were initiated into the world of meaning, both secular and religious, by a language foreign to the country where they now lived.

Most Helvetia children who started school between 1870 and 1900 understood virtually no English at the beginning of first grade. Their parents, of course, realized that learning English was necessary in America. Some attended English classes themselves in order to better understand the language. Teaching the children English, however, was considered the proper role of the school, not that of the family or church. The school system alone was responsible for initiating the children into American culture and language, while other facets of life continued to require the use of German. The students learned to speak English at school and German at home, just as their parents had learned to speak High German at school, and their local dialect at home. [18]

As the next generation reached school age after 1900, English became more common in the home. The parents were now bilingual, and the changes introduced by the timber boom made it apparent that fluent English was necessary to get ahead in the world. The events of World War I only reinforced this observation. Nonetheless, a knowledge of German was still necessary to fully understand church services and to converse easily with grandparents throughout most of the years between world wars. Although few children born during this time became truly bilingual, they learned some basic German skills at church and in the extended family.

As a result of these changes, the need for English language use in church became increasingly apparent. The transition, however, was anything but abrupt. Beginning in the 1920s, one of the German pastors introduced catechismal instruction in English as the most practical way to teach an understanding of the church. He also began the practice of preaching every other Sunday in English, even though a number of older members did not attend those services. Genevieve Hofer, a Helvetia schoolteacher who grew up during the transition, recalled that the innovation was continued throughout the 1930s. "There was still a great many people who didn't speak that much English," she explained. "The grandparents Aegerters, the grandparents Bürkis and many of the people understood English, but did not understand that much." For this reason, occasional German services were continued up to World War II. [19]

During and after the war, it became virtually impossible for the classis to supply bilingual ministers to Helvetia. After a long vacancy at the Helvetia Church, the Synod of the Reformed Church accepted an offer from the Presbyterian Church for a "cooperative pastorate" in the Helvetia area. The position was filled by Rev. Robert K. Robinson, a recent graduate of the Presbyterian Union Theological Seminary at Richmond, Virginia. During 1945 and 1946, Robinson worked at several churches in the area, finding his ministry at Helvetia well received by most of the congregation. [20]

In September 1946, the Helvetia church received a letter from the Presbyterian Board of Home Missions stating that they were satisfied with the

Teaching was one of the few professions open to women at the turn of the century and these second-generation Helvetia women were proud of their positions. By using their skills in the community, they made the transition from the Swiss German to English language much easier for beginning students. Left to right, Mary Huber, Nell Daetwyler, Ruth Fahrner, Lena Haslebacher. Date and photographer unknown.

arrangement, but asking if the church would consider a "closer relationship." Translated, this meant that the way was clear for becoming a Presbyterian body if the congregation so desired. It was an agonizing decision which led to much discussion and aroused deep feelings on both sides of the issue. Planning for the future was pitted against seventy years of tradition—a tradition that for the older members both rooted them in their native land and symbolized the faith that had brought them through the difficult years of settlement. In the end, however, most were in favor of making the change. The congregation

The 1901 confirmation class at the Reformed Church with Rev. Arthur Steinebrey. The elevated pulpit behind the group was removed after the church became Presbyterian. Courtesy Della Metzener.

voted fifty-four to five to accept the Presbyterian offer, and on May 22, 1947, the Southeast Ohio Synod began a smooth transfer of responsibilities to the Presbyterian Church of the United States.[21]

The vote to move ahead, although spurred by the younger members of the church, was not a vote against the German Reformed tradition. It was, rather, a vote for the future. For only the Presbyterian Church, with its large national network and monetary sharing systems, could have continued to help support such a small congregation in an area of such low population density.

The transfer signaled, in a dramatic way, the end of an era in Helvetia's history. The last surviving institution of Swiss German culture had given way to the Americanization process. It was a process begun when the first Helvetian child walked into a small, one-room school, began to learn a new language, and understood what it meant to be born on American soil. The isolation of the community and its strong cultural domain slowed the process in the early years of the settlement, but when the domain was invaded by the timber boom and the anti-German sentiment of World War I, the process accelerated. Finally, even the church yielded to the need for using the language of the adopted country.

The custom of speaking German in the home remained until all the native speakers had died, and in some cases, longer. Out of respect for their parents and grandparents, families continued to use the old language alongside the new. "We wouldn't be allowed to say an English word in front of my grandmother," remembered one Helvetia woman. "They were very proud of their language." Later, when her husband was asked why he did not teach his children German, he replied, "We live in America, so we'll just talk English and be done with it."[22]

Both the church and the family had provided for their members a strong sense of continuity amid the changes and adjustments inherent in immigrant life. They had fostered stability and cohesion in the community, while at the same time offering creative responses to a changing way of life. In this way, they were not simply reacting to the forces of change, but learning to control and shape them to fit the needs of the community and its members.

Chapter 7

The Community in Context

O F THE VARIOUS PLACES in the United States that Swiss immigrants chose to settle in the nineteenth century, the slopes of the central Appalachians were among the most isolated and undeveloped. Those who ventured into the region were few, but they came for very understandable reasons. Land was easily obtainable, and it could be lived on and paid for within a short period of time. There was an opportunity to own not only large amounts of property, but to live the life of self-sufficient farmers and craftsmen among people of a similar cultural background. These opportunities were highly valued by the land-conscious Swiss and Germans who were often deeply attached to their heritage. It was also a way of life offering an alternative to the factory jobs and labor problems of an industrial system, which at the time had very little respect for the health and well-being of the worker. To the immigrants, the mountains offered a home away from the pressures of rapid adjustment to American culture—a buffer zone, where change was slowed to a more human pace and the feelings of "culture shock" were greatly decreased.

These opportunities could have perhaps been duplicated in a number of locations east of the frontier line, but the immigrant rarely had all the information in front of him. Those who came to Helvetia and the other Appalachian settlements responded to the advertising and exaggerated claims of land speculators in the region. Swiss agents, who were backed by local lawyers, judges, and legislators painted an all too optimistic and often false picture of boundless economic development. They skillfully used their positions to create an image of trust, while playing on the immigrants' hopes and ambitions of success.

When expectations were not met, some of the settlers became disillusioned and moved away, but the majority stayed to help build enduring communities. At Helvetia, the practical ingenuity of the immigrants, together with their excellent health and stamina, was vital to the success of the settlement. Nonetheless, the mountains imposed a prolonged period of subsistence living, which generated little cash or opportunity for upward mobility. Particularly between 1869 and 1900, Helvetia realized to a large degree the attributes of anthropologist Robert Redfield's "genuine little community"—those of distinctiveness, smallness, homogeneity, and all-pervading self-sufficiency.[1] It enjoyed a wide participation in town affairs, no extremes of wealth or poverty, and no clearly defined social classes. It was, in general, a healthy, peaceful place to live, although a very difficult one in which to make a living.

Few people would dispute that, given the soil and topography of Randolph County, the settlers worked a minor agricultural miracle. They were able to develop a way of life that gave them security in raising large families and meeting their needs. Yet, several factors beyond their control spoiled what might have been the ultimate fruits of these labors. A combination of rugged mountains which impeded transportation, a development faith that gave up control of large land areas to outside interests, and the long distance to economic centers created a kind of economic island of the central Appalachians. Consequently, the lively farmers' markets of eastern Pennsylvania, for example, never had a chance to develop for the mountain communities like Helvetia. In Pennsylvania and other areas, the German and Swiss farmers were near enough to large towns and cities to make the sale of their fresh produce a lucrative business, but in the remote mountains this was an impossibility. One of the ironies of the Swiss migration to the region is that the same ambitions and creative energies which spawned wealth in Lancaster County, Pennsylvania, or Green County, Wisconsin, were frustrated in the mountains of West Virginia, Kentucky, and Tennessee.

The mountains, on the other hand, were extremely rich in natural resources: water, water power, coal, timber, and in some cases, oil and natural gas. The extraction of these resources provided jobs, but it did not bring long-term prosperity either to the workers or the region. Outside corporations drew most of the profits and raw materials away from their source, profits which would normally be reinvested in the area and raw materials that could be further refined by local businesses. Such extractive industries were also destabilizing, because when they moved to a new location the economy collapsed behind them. This cycle of boom and bust is a common feature of what has been called a "colonial economy" in the central Appalachians.[2] It is so named because resources are extracted from one area to the advantage of another, while the "colony" reaps few, if any, of the economic and social benefits. Helvetia, like the hundreds of other small towns in the region, was inescapably tied to these trends. When farming ceased to be a viable livelihood, the only alternatives were to migrate or work in the sawmills and coal mines. As owners of coal and timberlands (usually no more than 100 to 300 acres), Helvetians did receive temporary income from their resources, but few people received a large return on the sale of timber and coal or from the wages paid to cut and mine them. Thus, like most other West Virginians, Helvetians became members of the rank and file of a larger economic and industrial system. The net effect of this change from a self-reliant agriculture to extractive industries was to remove the means of production from the community and place them with outside interests. As a result, the community became increasingly vulnerable to destabilizing economic trends and lost much of its ability to control its own destiny.

The settling of Helvetia is not unique as a case of Swiss immigration and migration to the central Appalachians. The other Swiss German communities founded in West Virginia, Kentucky, and Tennessee during the last half of the nineteenth century have much in common. They were extremely isolated from economic centers and suffered the same lack of planning and turmoil as a result of speculative land sales. They attracted a very similar type of person, who lived in small, family clusters dispersed

over mountainous, rural neighborhoods. These settlements were different in character from Swiss colonies such as New Glarus, Wisconsin. In contrast to colonies, which were usually well-planned, deliberate emigrations of whole groups, the Appalachian settlements were aggregations of settlers who came together largely in response to advertising campaigns mounted in the United States. In Helvetia, Bernstadt, and Grütli, this involved the work of agents who so misled people that they were eventually banished from the settlements. The notable exception was John Kaserman, the founder of Belvidere, Tennessee. [3]

Kaserman was born in New Philadelphia, Ohio, the son of Swiss parents. After the Civil War he moved to the mountains of Tennessee, where according to Walter Kollmorgen, a researcher for the U.S. Department of Agriculture, he was responsible for attracting nearly every German and Swiss family who settled in the area. Unlike Charles Lutz (in Helvetia), Otto Brunner (in Bernstadt), and Peter Staub (in Grütli), Kaserman was himself an earnest farmer who gained his living from the soil, rather than at the expense of his fellow Swiss. He was, by contrast, well accepted and successful in the community.[4]

The aggregation of Swiss in the mountains also fostered a different community structure. Unlike colonies where land ownership was usually closely regulated, in the Appalachian settlements, a settler could own as much land as he wanted and could choose the tract or tracts he preferred. This led to decentralized communities where people were often separated by several miles or by steep mountain ridges. Clusters of families formed a kind of rural neighborhood as one-room schools, kinship relationships, and economic ties developed among them. Such clusters were particularly apparent around Helvetia and around the Saaner Colony as additional families filtered into Kentucky in the 1880s. [5]

The people themselves were often quite similar in background and experience. In the cases of Bernstadt, Grütli, Alpina, and Adolph, a large portion of the settlers arrived directly from Switzerland, although later arrivals usually came from other sections of the United States. They were predominantly German-speaking, Protestant, skilled in a wide array of trades, and often originally from Switzerland's largest canton, Bern. [6]

In farming endeavors, the Swiss in Franklin County, Kentucky, and probably in the other settlements, were as successful as those in Helvetia, if not more so. Kollmorgen reported that John Kaserman was "one of the boldest, best read, and most ingenious farmers to settle in the County," even though he had not previously farmed. The Swiss were credited as the ones who introduced the reaper, binder, grain drill, horse rake, two-row cultivator, windmill, manure spreader, and cream separator into Franklin County. In agronomy they brought red clover, crimson clover, and alfalfa into the crop rotation cycle and were noted as a group who worked cooperatively. Kollmorgen observed the same lifestyle and

work structure in Belvidere as in Helvetia. "The industry, thrift, and varied activities of the men outside the house," he reported, "were matched by the women in house and garden. From the first, these people have maintained large, well-kept gardens, producing a great variety of vegetables and foods." [7]

The maintenance of Swiss social and cultural traditions was a common feature of all the settlements. Grütli, Tennessee, for example, a community founded in 1869 under severe conditions of terrain and lack of planning, organized the inevitable mutual aid society, brass band, and riflery club. Favorite pastimes included dancing, playing *Jass*, and drinking wine. At school, English was spoken three days a week, German on the other two. However, about 1900, the County Board of Education disallowed the use of German in public school. [8]

On Sundays at Grütli, church met in the schoolhouse. The congregation joined the German Reformed Church of America, and although they had no full-time minister, they were visited once a month by a pastor from Belvidere, Tennessee. Grütli also held an agricultural fair as early as the 1870s and organized a *Landwirtschaftverein* or farmer's association, to facilitate cooperative farming activities. In 1902, it protested the dropping of German from school, and in 1910 advertised for more immigrants, because it felt the settlement was getting into the hands of too many Americans. Here, too, the most vital Swiss societies provided a sense of continuity and tradition well into the twentieth century. [9]

Although more research needs to be done, the settlement of Swiss and Germans in the central Appalachians can now be seen in clearer focus. While it was once thought that these tiny settlements represented only the ability of clever land speculators to trick a few unsuspecting immigrants into buying useless land, it is now apparent that it represented an opportunity to enter an open community where sacrifice and difficulties were endured for the many benefits offered by a small, homogeneous settlement. Here, the Swiss and Germans from various cantons and provinces were able to sustain the traditions they most valued. Their predisposition to hard work and openness to new techniques made them successful when the odds were against them. From a land of rugged mountains, they came equipped with varied skills, allowing them to meet the challenges of the New World head on, and to remain, for the duration of their often long lives, a part of the communities they cherished.

Chapter 8

Helvetia Life 1950–2009

Helvetia's flavor is captured in its signage, 2009. Photo by David H. Sutton.

Helvetia signage, 2009. Photo by David H. Sutton.

Helvetia signage, 2009. Photo by David H. Sutton.

99

Helvetia signage, 2009. Photo by David H. Sutton.

Helvetia Folk Dancers c. 1950. Helvetia Archives.

Louis Lehmann, a well-known local farmer, 1978. Photo by Norton Gusky.

Helvetia Folk Dancers, 1979. Photo by Norton Gusky.

Woody Higginbotham and Micky Biggs lead a twirl at a 2007 folk dance performance. Photographer unknown.

Woody Higginbotham and Joe McInroy play the alp horns, while Alexander and Norm Biggs demonstrate the age old art of flag throwing in the Meadow, 2007. Photographer unknown.

Dancing and frolicking at the Fair, 1981. Photo by Norton Gusky.

Anne Mailloux (left) and Betty Daetwyler Biggs play the old waltzes and polkas at the Fair, 1979. Photo by Norton Gusky.

Local artist Joe McInroy demonstrates his technique, 2000. Photo by Dave Whipp.

The main street and store, August 1978. Photo by Norton Gusky.

Main street, 2009. Photo by David H. Sutton.

Helvetia store, post office, and Daetwyler family home, 1979. Photo by Norton Gusky.

Interior of the store and post office, 1979. Photo by Norton Gusky.

The first footbridge leading from the Historic Square to the Star Band Hall and Daetwyler family home, 1979. Photo by Norton Gusky.

Star Band Hall and Daetwyler family home, 2009. Photo by David H. Sutton.

View of the village from above the church, May 1979. Photo by Norton Gusky.

A few livestock still grace the village meadows, 2007. Photo by David H. Sutton.

A group of *Fastnacht* revelers begin the march from the Hütte to the Community Hall, 2004. Photo by Steve Shaluta.

Fastnacht dance, 2004. Photo by Steve Shaluta.

Burning Old Man Winter at *Fastnacht*, 2007. Photo by Dave Whipp.

Fastnacht costume, 2009. Photo by Dave Whipp.

118

Helvetia Star Band Hall, 2007. Photo by Dave Whipp.

The Community Hall, designed for dances, ramp dinners, the Fair, and many events, 2008. Photo by Dave Whipp.

Beekeeper Inn Bed and Breakfast, 2007. Photo by David H. Sutton.

Settler's Cabin Museum, 2007. Photo by David H. Sutton.

Some early community artifacts in the museum, 2008. Photo by Dave Whipp.

The old Huber Inn, later home of Eleanor Mailloux, 2007. Photo by David H. Sutton.

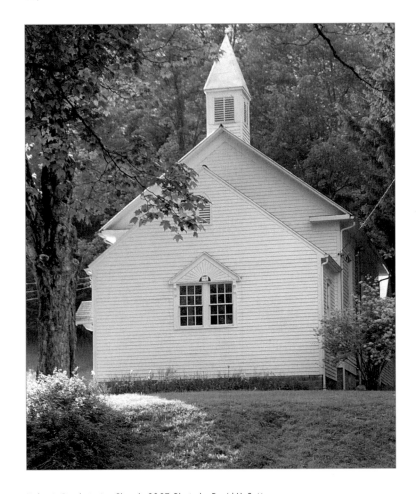

Helvetia Presbyterian Church, 2007. Photo by David H. Sutton.

Emma Jo Betler making cheese in her home, 1950. Helvetia Archives.

Cheesemaking is an old tradition still alive in Helvetia, 2007. Photo by Dave Whipp.

Fred Burky playing the fiddle for a local dance, 2007. Photo by Dave Whipp.

Mary and Jeff McNeal enjoy a bountiful community dinner, 2007. Photo by Dave Whipp.

Leroy Gain prepares potatoes for the Ramp Dinner, 2008. Photo by Dave Whipp.

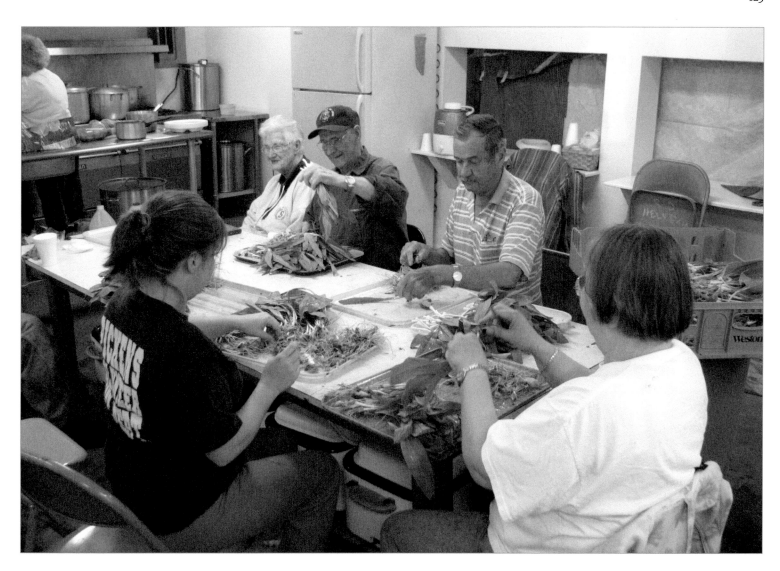

A large group of helpers, some shown here, prepare the ramps days in advance, 2008. Photo by Dave Whipp.

Anna Merkli McNeal on her 100th birthday, October 1980. Ella Betler in the background. Photo by Norton Gusky.

Eleanor Mailloux takes a moment at the Hütte with granddaughters Anna (left) and Clara, 2008. Photo by Dave Whipp.

View of the Meadow from the Hütte porch, 2009. Photo by David H. Sutton.

The Hütte Restaurant as it appeared summer 2009. Photo by David H. Sutton.

134

Interior dining area of the Hütte. Photo by David H. Sutton.

Interior dining area of the Hütte. Photo by Steve Shaluta.

Construction for the public water system, summer 2009. Photo by David H. Sutton.

Notes

Preface Notes

1. Guy Metraux, "Social and Cultural Aspects of Swiss Immigration into the United States in the Nineteenth Century," (PhD Dissertation, Yale University, 1949), p. 54.

Chapter 1 Notes

1. Leo Schelbert, ed., *New Glarus 1845–1970: The Making of a Swiss American Town*, (Kommissionsverlag Tschudi & Co. AG. Glarus 1970), p. 5.
2. William Martin, *Switzerland from Roman Times to the Present*, (New York and Washington: Praeger Press, English Ed., 1971); Kurt Mayer, *The Population of Switzerland*, p. 29; Leo Schelbert, "Swiss Migration to America: The Swiss Mennonites," p. 96.
3. Guy Metraux, "Social and Cultural Aspects of Swiss Immigration into the United States in the Nineteenth Cen-tury," p. 24; Kurt Mayer, *The Population of Switzerland*, p. 203; Leo Schelbert, "The Swiss Migration to America: The Swiss Mennonites," p. 97. NOTE: In the canton of Lucerne alone, 2,000 farms were auctioned off during the 1880s. (Otto Kaufman, *Das Neue Ländliche Bodenrecht der Schweiz* (St. Gallen: 1944), cited in Metraux, p. 27); See also, Mayer, p. 204 for statistics of civilian emigration from Switzerland for the period 1798 to 1941, and additional tables on the destination and occupational characteristics of Swiss emigrants. Mayer, Schelbert, and Metraux all contain brief discussions of the many problems of obtaining accurate statistics.
4. Stephan Thernstrom, ed., *Harvard Encyclopedia of American Ethnic Groups*, (Cambridge: Harvard University Press, 1980).
5. Guy Metraux, "Social and Cultural Aspects of Swiss Immigration," pp. 17, 28; See Heinz K. Meier, *The United States and Switzerland in the Nineteenth Century*,

(The Hague: Mouton & Co., 1963), pp. 105–122, for a careful discussion of the diplomatic problems of pauper emigration.

6. Ibid., p. 10.

7. Ibid., pp. 11, 12.

8. Elizabeth Cometti, "Swiss Immigration to West Virginia: A Case Study," *Mississippi Valley Historical Review* (Vol. XLVII, No.1, June 1960), p. 75.

9. Ibid., p. 78; Marcus Lee Hansen, *The Atlantic Migration 1607-1860*, (Cambridge: Harvard University Press, 1948), p. 291.

10. Ibid., p. 53.

11. Ibid., p. 54.

12. Gerald Arlettaz, *Etudes et Sources, Emigration et colonisation suisses en Amerique 1815-1918*, p. 54; Adelrich Steinach, *Geschichte und Leben der Schweizer Colonien in den Vereinigten Staaten von Nord-Amerika*, (New York: By the Author, 1889), pp. 152–171.

13. Adelrich Steinach, *Geschichte und Leben der Schweizer Colonien*, pp. 158, 159; C. E. Lutz, Bern, to Jonathan M. Bennett, Weston, West Virginia, 26 July 1874. Jonathan M. Bennett Collection, West Virginia and Regional History Collection, West Virginia University; Paul Schenk, *The Colony Bernstadt in Laurel County, Kentucky at the Beginning of Its Sixth Year*, Translation by S. A. Mory (London, Kentucky: The Sentinel Echo, 1940); Guy Metraux, "Social and Cultural Aspects of Swiss Immigration," p. 141.

14. Adelrich Steinach, *Geschichte und Leben der Schweizer Colonien*, p. 161.

15. Ibid., p. 161; Gerald Arlettaz, *Etudes et Sources, Emigration et colonization suisses en Amerique 1815-1918*, p. 54. NOTE: Louisville had been a center for Swiss for many years and in 1884 it received a Swiss consulate.

16. Francis H. Jackson, "The German Swiss Settlement of Grütli, Tennessee," (Masters Thesis, Vanderbilt University, Nashville, Tennessee, 1933).

17. Francis H. Jackson, ibid.; Adelrich Steinach, *Geschichte und Leben der Schweizer Colonien*, pp. 163–164.

18. Alderich Steinach, ibid., pp. 165, 168, 170; Gerald Arlettaz, *Etudes de Sources*, p. 54; Walter M. Kollmorgen, *The German Swiss in Franklin County Tennessee: A Study of the Significance of Cultural Considerations in Farming Enterprises*. (Washington, D.C.; Department of Agriculture, 1940); Guy Metraux, "Social and Cultural Aspects of Swiss Immigration," pp. 144, 147.

19. Alderich Steinach, *Geschichte und Leben der Schweizer Colonien*, p. 152.

20. Otto Brunner, *Die Auswanderung nach den Vereingten Staaten Nordamerikas, amerikanische landwirtschaftliche Verhältnisse und ein neues Ansiedlungs-project*, (Bern: Kommissions – Verlag von Huber & Cie., 1881); United States Geographical Survey Topographical Map, Kanawha Falls edition, 1901.

21. James Comstock, ed., *West Virginia Heritage Encyclopedia*, (Richwood, West Virginia: The Editor, 1976), Vol. 2, p. 2266; Gerald Arlettaz, *Etudes de Sources*, p. 54. NOTE: Since research for this book was completed, Erdmann Schmocker, a researcher of Swiss place names in the United States, has documented the existence of the town of Newberne, W. Va. in Gilmer County. This may be on the site where, according to Karl Lutz, Jonathan M. Bennett owned 70,000 acres that he intended to sell to homesteaders. This land is mentioned in letters

from Lutz to Bennett, 13 December 1870, 23 January 1871, and 26 July 1874.

22. Guy Metraux, "Social and Cultural Influences of Swiss Immigration," p. 114 ff.; Leo Schelbert, ed., *New Glarus 1845-1970: The Making of a Swiss American Town*, (Kommissionsverlag Tschudi & Co. AG. Glarus 1970).

Chapter 2 Notes

1. Otis K. Rice, *The Allegheny Frontier*, (Lexington: University Press of Kentucky, 1970), pp. xi, 1, 66.

2. Ibid., pp. 153, 167

3. John Paul von Grueningen, ed., *The Swiss in the United States*, (Madison, Wisconsin: The Swiss American Historical Society, 1940), pp. 26, 113.

4. John Hitz Jr. "Bericht des schweizerischen General-konsuls über das Jahr 1875" Record Group E 2400/ Washington D.C. 1-4, pp. 303-312. Swiss National Archive, Bern, Switzerland.

5. Charles E. Lutz to G. D. Camden, 13 May 1871.

6. Charles E. Lutz, "Helvetia, Randolph County, West Virginien"; Gray's New Topographic of Virginia and West Virginia for 1879; M. Wood White's County and District Map of the State of West Virginia for 1875; Colton's Virginia and West Virginia, 1869; United States Geographic Survey Topographic Map, Pickens Quadrangle, 1977, West Virginia and Regional History Collection, Morgantown, West Virginia; *Ninth Census of the United States, Statistics of the Population, Tables I-VIII*, Washington: GPO, 1872. NOTE: Union Township, where the settlement was to be located, was in 1870 the most uninhabited of Randolph County's nine townships, with a population of only 340 people.

7. Eugene Daetwyler, [Mrs.] Emil Metzener, Annie Teuscher, *The Story of Helvetia Community*, (Morgantown: The Agriculture Extension Division, West Virginia University, 1923).

8. Anne Lorentz, "Swiss Village Thrives in West Virginia Hills," (*Clarksburg Telegram*, September 30, 1930.) NOTE: A brief visit made by the author to Anne Lorentz Miller during 1979 revealed that Mrs. Asper was an excellent source. "She was full of fire when she described it (the founding of Helvetia)," Miller said. "Her recollection was perfect."

9. Ibid.

10. Ninth Census of the United States 1870, Union Township, Randolph County, West Virginia; Bürger Register der Stadt Lenzburg, Band I, Seite 158, State Archive of the Canton of Aargau, Aarau, Switzerland; Frieda Halder to Eleanor Mailloux, 5 June 1980.

11. Ninth Census of the United States 1870; Helvetia Evangelical Reformed Church, Family Register, Book II, p. 228. NOTE: There is no evidence that the sixth committee member, Xavier Holzweg, settled or bought land in Helvetia. The surveyor, John B. Isler, bought land, but apparently did not settle on it. He lived in New Hope, Maryland.

12. "The Early Pioneers of Helvetia," The Werner and Alma Burky Collection, Helvetia Community Archive, Helvetia, West Virginia; Anne Lorentz, "Swiss Village Thrives in West Virginia Hills." NOTE: In his "Sixth Annual Report to the West Virginia Legislature for the Year of 1869," Commissioner of Immigration, J. H. Diss Debar, takes full credit for the founding of Helvetia. Since all evidence, including Mrs. Asper's eye-witness account, is contrary to this claim, it is

likely that Debar conveniently included Helvetia in the report to bolster his position with the Legislature. The name "Helvetia" is the original Latin for Switzerland, still used today for many designations, including the identification of Swiss postage stamps and currency.

13. David Sutton, Interview with Ella Betler, Helvetia, West Virginia, 26 April 1979. Available in *Goldenseal Magazine* (April–June 1980), p.23; Guy S. Metraux, "Social and Cultural Aspects of Swiss Immigration into the United Sates in the Nineteenth Century," (PhD Dissertation, Yale University, 1949), pp. 54, 55.

14. C. E. Lutz to J. M. Bennett, 30 September 1877, Jonathan M. Bennett Collection, West Virginia and Regional History Collection, Morgantown, West Virginia; Ninth Census of the United States 1870.

15. "Manual des Obergerichts der Republik Bern über Kriminal and Polizei Sentenzen" Band 40, 1839–1840, p. 284; "Geldstags Protokoll Vermögen und Schulden des Karl Emanuel Lutz von Bern," pp. 21, 47. Bern Cantonal Archive, Bern, Switzerland. NOTE: Lutz's home, which once stood at 62a/62b Arbergasse, was valued in 1840 at 19,000 Swiss Francs.

16. "Manual des Obergerichts," ibid., pp. 285–296.

17. Ibid., pp. 308, 309.

18. "Geldstages Protokoll Vermögen und Schulden des Karl Emanuel Lutz von Bern," pp. 26, 27.

19. Elizabeth Cometti, "Swiss Immigration to West Virginia: A Case Study," *Mississippi Valley Historical Review*, (Vol. XLVII, No. 1, June 1960).

20. Elkins Randolph County Courthouse, *Deed Book C*, p. 295; *Deed Book E*, pp. 164–165; John Hitz Jr., "Bericht des schweizerischen Generalkonsuls über das Jahr 1875,"

Record Group E 2400/Washington, D.C. 1–4, p. 303.

21. Elkins Randolph County Courthouse, *Deed Book B*, pp. 489–490; John Hitz Jr., ibid., p. 303; NOTE: Lutz wrote J. M. Bennett that the settlers received their land free of charge from Samuel Peugh with the conditions that they stay five years. This would go a long way toward explaining their quick move to the wilderness, but there is no other evidence for this claim. Oral accounts do not carry this tradition and deeds to the land indicated the settlers paid Peugh from three to five dollars an acre.

22. Elkins Randolph County Courthouse, *Deed Book C*, p. 217; John Hitz Jr. "Bericht des schweizerischen Generalkonsuls über das Jahr 1875," p. 305.

23. Harvey Mitchell Rice, *The Life of Jonathan M. Bennett: A Study of the Virginias in Transition*, (Chapel Hill: North Carolina University Press, 1943); George W. Atkinson, ed., *Bench and Bar of West Virginia*, (Charleston, West Virginia: Virginian Law Book Company, 1919), pp. 60–67. NOTE: Other West Virginia lawyers, legislators, and land speculators involved in Helvetia land deals include M. W. Harrison, W. L. Ward, David Goff, and Jonathan Arnold.

24. C. E. Lutz to J. M. Bennett, 18 September 1870.

25. Ibid., 1 January 1871.

26. Ibid., 7 March 1871.

27. C. E. Lutz to Col. (John) Hoffman, 26 October 1870; C. E. Lutz to J. M. Bennett, 13 December 1870; 23 January 1871.

28. C. E. Lutz to G. D. Camden, 26 May 1871, Gidean D. Camden Collection, West Virginia and Regional History Collection, Morgantown, West Virginia; Harvey M. Rice, *The Life of Jonathan M. Bennett*, p. 173.

29. C. E. Lutz to G. D. Camden, 13 May 1871.

30. Ibid.

31. For a history of Pickens, West Virginia, see: Arnold E. and Rosemary Smith Nelson, *Haven in the Hardwood*, (Parsons, West Virginia: McClain Printing Company, 1971); Elkins Randolph County Courthouse, *Deed Book D*, p. 645.

32. C. E. Lutz to G. D. Camden, 5 June 1871.

33. C. E. Lutz to J. M. Bennett, 24 April 1876; 13 September 1872.

34. C. E. Lutz to G. D. Camden, 13 September 1872.

35. Ibid., 10 October 1873; C. E. Lutz to G. D. Camden, 16 October 1872.

36. Ulrich Müller to J. M. Bennett, 5 January 1872; John Hitz Jr., "Bericht des schweizerischen Generalkonsuls über das Jahr 1875," p. 306; Gottlieb Betler to J. M. Bennett, 25 March 1875 (1876).

37. C. E. Lutz to J. M. Bennett, 10 January 1874; *Kontrolle über die Wohnungen der Studierenden, 1834–1850*, BB IIIb 2701; *Polizei Abteilung: Schriftenwesen - Paesse No. 3, 1847–1852*, 348a 2/2, Cantonal Archive of Bern, Bern, Switzerland.

38. C. E. Lutz to J. M. Bennett, 16 July 1874.

39. Eugene Lutz to G. D. Camden, 21 June 1878; Paul Schenk, *The Colony Bernstadt in Laurel County, Kentucky at the Beginning of the Sixth Year*, (London, Ky.: The Author, 1886); David Sutton, Interview with Anna Merkli McNeal, Helvetia, West Virginia, 25 February 1979.

40. C. E. Lutz to G. D. Camden, 9 July 1875.

41. Ibid., 18 June 1875,

42. John Hitz Jr., "Bericht des schweizerischen Generalkonsuls über das Jahr 1875," pp. 303–308.

43. Ibid.

44. C. E. Lutz to J. M. Bennett, 17 August 1877.

45. Ibid.

46. Ibid., 6 April 1878; 9 February 1878.

47. Elizabeth Cometti, "Swiss Immigration to West Virginia: A Case Study," pp. 77, 78.

48. Hu Maxwell, *The History of Randolph County, West Virginia*, (Morgantown, West Virginia: Acme Publishing Co., 1898.) p. 297; Elizabeth Cometti, "Swiss Immigration to West Virginia: A Case Study," p. 84; Adelrich Steinach, *Geschichte und Leben der Schweizer Colonien in den Vereinigten Staaten von Nord-Amerika*, (New York: The Author, 1889), p. 153.

49. "Deutsche Colonie Helvetia, West Virginia," March 1878, (Advertising flyer published by the Helvetia Land Committee, Fred. Wälchli Corresponding Secretary), Schweizer Gesandtschaft in Washington – Einwanderungs gesetze bis 1895. *Schweizer Kolonien und Ansiedlungen den Vereinigten Staaten*, Swiss National Archive, Bern, Switzerland.

50. John Hitz Jr., "Bericht des schweizerischen Generalkonsuls über das Jahr 1875," p. 304.

51. "Deutsche Colonie Helvetia, West Virginia," March 1878.

52. Ibid.

Chapter 3 Notes

1. John Hitz Jr., "Bericht des schweizerischen Generalkonsuls über das Jahr 1875," AF, E 2400/Washington, D.C. 104. Swiss National Archive. NOTE: This report contains an attachment submitted by Dr. C. F. Stucky giving information about Helvetia.; Tenth Census of the United States: 1880, Union Township, Randolph County, West Virginia.

2. Ninth Census of the United States 1870, Union Township, Randolph County, West Virginia; Tenth Census of the United States 1880; Records of the Helvetia Evangelical Reformed Church, Family Register, Books I and II, 1873–ca. 1950.

3. John Hitz Jr., "Bericht"; Tenth Census of the United States 1880.

4. William Martin, *Switzerland from Roman Times to the Present*, (New York and Washington, Praeger Press, 1971); "Deutsche Colonie Helvetia, West Virginia," March 1878. (Advertising flyer published by the Helvetia Land Committee, Fred. Wälchli Corresponding Secretary), Schweizer Gesandtschaft in Washington –Einwanderungsgesetze bis 1895.

5. Ninth Census of the United States 1870; Tenth Census of the United States 1880; Records of the Helvetia Evangelical Reformed Church, Family Register Books I and II.

6. Bürgerregister der Gemeinde Wettingen, Band II, Seiten 87, 223, Cantonal Archive of Aargau; Troy B. Wilmoth, "Swiss Communities in Randolph County," MA Thesis, West Virginia University, 1937, p. 7; David H. Sutton, Interview with Anna Merkli McNeal, 22 January 1979.

7. Troy B. Wilmoth, ibid., p. 8

8. Ibid.

9. Ibid., p. 9

10. Tenth Census; ibid.

11. John Hitz Jr., "Bericht."

12. See Appendix 4 for sources and a detailed discussion of how life expectancies were calculated.

13. John Hitz Jr., "Bericht"; Tenth Census of the United States 1880.

14. John Hitz Jr., "Bericht"; David H. Sutton, Interview with Anna Merkli McNeal, 22 January 1979; Historical Photos of Helvetia.

15. Eugene Daetwyler, et al., *The Story of Helvetia Community*, (Morgantown, West Virginia: The Agricultural Extension Service, 1923); John Hitz Jr., "Bericht"; Twelfth Census of the United States 1900.

16. Eugene Daetwyler, et al., *The Story of Helvetia Community*; Tenth Census of the United States 1880. NOTE: The Blum Sanitorium was purchased by the Herman Koerner family as a residence and hotel. It was located on the bank downstream of the community hall where today a small cement-block house stands.; Tenth Census of the United States 1880.

17. John Hitz Jr., "Bericht"; David H. Sutton, Interview with Eugene Daetwyler, 18 February 1979; Reconstructed Tax Map of Helvetia, Randolph County Courthouse; C. E. Lutz to G. D. Camden, 24 April 1871; Mrs. Ruth Williamson to David H. Sutton, 6 September 1979.

18. David H. Sutton, Interview with Eugene Daetwyler, 18 February 1979, and Anna Merkli McNeal, 22 January 1979.

19. Ibid., Interviews with Mary Huber Marti, 13 July 1979, and 27 September 1979; Eugene Daetwyler, *The Story of Helvetia Community*, 1923; John Hitz Jr., "Bericht."

20. Tenth Census, ibid.; David H. Sutton, Interviews with Helen Sutton, 29 December 1979; Eleanor F. Mailloux, 30 January 1980; Mary Morris, 18 November 1979; Anna Merkli McNeal, 26 January 1979.

21. This Webster County Settlement may be referred to in Alderich Steinach's *Gerschichte und Leben der Schweizer Kolonien in den Vereingten Staaten von Nord-Amerika*

(New York, 1889), as New St. Gallen, but in local tradition, the cluster did not take a name.

22. Tenth Census of the United States 1880.

Chapter 4 Notes

1. George Sharpe, *Land Judging: Learning to Know Your Soil* (Agricultural Extension Service, West Virginia University, Circular 386) cited in Atje Partadiredja, "Helvetia, West Virginia: A Study in Pioneer Development and Community Survival in Appalachia," (PhD Dissertation, University of Wisconsin, 1966), p. 96. (Hereafter cited as Partadiredja, "Helvetia")

2. Ibid.

3. John Hitz Jr., "Bericht des schweizerischen Generalkonsuls über das Jahr 1875," Record Group E 2400/ Washington, D.C. 1–4, pp. 309–310; David B. Reger, *West Virginia Geological Survey: Randolph County* (Morgantown, West Virginia University, 1931), p. 16. NOTE: Temperature and precipitation data after 1888 was collected at Pickens, W. Va., five miles from Helvetia.

4. Reger, ibid., pp. 16, 17.

5. The author's first-hand knowledge of property boundaries around Helvetia; David H. Sutton, Interviews with Mary Marti, 13 July 1979, and Helen Sutton, 29 December 1979, Helvetia, West Virginia.

6. John Hitz Jr., "Bericht," pp. 309, 310; *United States Census of Agriculture for 1900*, cited in Partadiredja, "Helvetia," p. 122. NOTE: Dr. Stucky's figures are obviously rounded. They are probably rounded upward in order to make a good appearance in his report to the Swiss Consul General.

7. John Hitz Jr., ibid.; "Deutsche Colonie Helvetia, West Virginia," March 1878. Flyer published by Helvetia Land Committee; *Buckhannon Delta*, 25 March 1880.

8. John Hitz Jr., "Bericht," pp. 309, 310.

9. Walter M. Kollmorgen, *The German-Swiss in Franklin County, Tennessee: A Study of the Significance of Cultural Considerations in Farming Enterprises* (Washington: U.S. Dept. of Agriculture, June 1940), p. 30; David H. Sutton, Interview with Ella Betler, 26 April 1979; and Interview with Eleanor Mailloux and Max Schneider, 19 February 1984, Helvetia, West Virginia.

10. Historical photos of Helvetia show the prevalence of farm machinery and the large variety of plants that were grown. Machines and tools are also discussed in an interview with Edward A. Sutton, 7 January 1980, Helvetia, West Virginia; The general condition of native farms was mentioned by C. E. Lutz in his ad, "Helvetia, Randolph Co., West Virginien," March 1873. A bank barn is one in which the ground floor is dug into the ground for insulation and warmth.

11. David H. Sutton, Interview with Anna Zumbach Daetwyler, 9 November 1979, Montrose, West Virginia.

12. David H. Sutton, Interviews with Anna Merkli McNeal, 22 January 1979; Helen Sutton, 29 December 1979; Genevieve Hofer, 27 November 1979.

13. David H. Sutton, Interviews with Anna Merkli McNeal, 22 January 1979; and Edward A. Sutton, 7 January 1980.

14. David H. Sutton, Interviews with Edward A. Sutton, ibid.; and Edwin Ramsey, 7 June 1979.

15. Partadiredja, "Helvetia," p. 143. This data gathered by Partadiredja in 1965 tells us less than we would like to know. Some indication of what was and was not taxable

would have been helpful in evaluating the data. This, unfortunately is not possible since sometime between 1965 and 1983 these documents were either lost or destroyed at the Randolph County Courthouse.

16. Ibid.; Partadiredja, "Helvetia," p. 191.

17. Ibid., pp. 205–224; David H. Sutton, Interview with Ella Betler, 26 April 1979; Helvetia Farm Men's Club Minutes, Book II – 1922 to 1935, Helvetia Community Archive, Helvetia, West Virginia. NOTE: Partadiredja contains fairly detailed information on the various farm organizations and extension services offered in Helvetia during this time, drawn primarily from the reports filed by county extension agents.

18. Partadiredja, "Helvetia," pp. 210–212. NOTE: In 1934 lamb production went up to 900 lambs, but as a result of the Depression, the price went down to 7¢ per pound. There are no separate statistics for Helvetia after this date.

19. Ibid., pp. 216, 217.

20. David H. Sutton, Interview with Anna Merkli McNeal, 5 February 1979; and Anna Fischer, 11 October 1979.

21. David H. Sutton, Interview with Anna Zumbach Daetwyler, 9 November 1979; Helvetia Farm Men's Club Minutes, Book II – 1922 to 1935, pp. 184–85. 187, 233, 235–36. Helvetia Community Archive.

22. Partadiredja, "Helvetia," pp. 160–171.

23. David H. Sutton, Interview with Ella Betler, 26 April 1979.

24. "Randolph County Agent's Annual Report 1925 and 1935," cited in Partadiredja, p. 239; David H. Sutton, ibid.

25. Ibid.

26. David H. Sutton, Interview with Edward A. Sutton, 7 January 1980.

Chapter 5 Notes

1. John Alexander Williams, *West Virginia: A Bicentennial History*, (New York: W. W. Norton & Company Inc., 1976), pp. 115, 148–158.

2. *Randolph Enterprise*, 22 May 1895.

3. David H. Sutton, Interview with Mary Huber Marti, 27 September 1979.

4. David B. Reger, *West Virginia Geological Survey: Barbour, Upshur and the Western Portion of Randolph County* (Morgantown: West Virginia University, 1918); *Randolph Enterprise*, 3 August 1916; Atje Partadiredja, "Helvetia, West Virginia: A Study of Pioneer Development and Community Survival in the Appalachia" (PhD Dissertation, University of Wisconsin, 1966), p. 260. (Hereafter cited as Partadiredja, "Helvetia.")

5. Benjamin Holtkamp, "The German Evangelical Reformed Church at Helvetia, Randolph County, West Virginia" Typed manuscript, August 1, 1919. Helvetia Community Archive, Helvetia, West Virginia; David H. Sutton, Interview with Mary Huber Marti, 13 July 1979; Donald Teter, *Goin' Up Gandy: A History of the Dry Fork Region of Randolph and Tucker Counties, W. Va.*, (Parsons: McClain Printing Co., 1977).

6. David H. Sutton, Interview with Edwin Ramsey, 7 June 1979.

7. Ibid.

8. David H. Sutton, Interviews with Mary Huber Marti, 27 September 1979; Paul Daetwyler, 12 November 1979; Myrtle Bowersach Koerner, 17 February 1979.

9. David H. Sutton, Interviews with Anna Merkli Mc-Neal, 7 February 1979; Ella Betler, 26 April 1979; Partadiredja, "Helvetia," p. 180.

10. David H. Sutton, Interview with Ella Betler, 25 September 1979.

11. "Teuton Flag Cause of War in Helvetia," *The Weekly New Dominion*, Morgantown, 18 April 1917.

12. "Helvetia Correspondence," *Elkins Inter-Mountain*, 28 May 1917. NOTE: Although the article of 18 April 1917 is obviously exaggerated, it is clear that a small incident of some sort did occur. Most people interviewed about the subject did not remember it happening, however, Mrs. Anna Zumbach Daetwyler who lived in Helvetia at the time, substantiated that there was an incident. She did not remember the details.

13. Nettie Vass Davis, "Helvetia – West Virginia's Swiss Village," *The West Virginia Review*, (December 1934, Vol. 12), pp. 80, 81; John Alexander Williams, *West Virginia: A Bicentennial History* (New York: W. W. Norton & Company, 1976), p. 104.

14. Partadiredja, "Helvetia," p. 259; David H. Sutton, Interview with Edwin Ramsey, 7 June 1979.

15. Partadiredja, "Helvetia," pp. 105, 113, 116; Interviews with Ella Betler, 26 April 1979; Mary Huber Marti, 27 September 1979; Edwin Ramsey, ibid.

16. Partadiredja, "Helvetia," pp. 261, 262, 267–271. NOTE: Until 1933, Randolph County Schools were governed by the district they were in. Middle Fork District, where Helvetia was, had no power to exact severance or other direct revenue from the timber companies. Companies headquartered downstream, in Upshur County, contributed even less to the tax base. Although Helvetia and Pickens often attracted a resident doctor, until 1976, the nearest clinic or hospital was in Buckhannon, forty miles away.

17. "Serving West Virginia's Unique Swiss Community," *Employee Newspaper of the C&P Telephone Company of West Virginia*, (Vol. 1, No. 38), December 30, 1966.

18. Partadiredja, "Helvetia," p. 261.

19. Ibid., p. 265.

20. David H. Sutton, Interviews with Anna Merkli McNeal, 5 February 1979; Genevieve Hofer, 27 November 1979.

21. David H. Sutton, Interview with Edward A. Sutton, 7 January 1980. NOTE: For further reading concerning what has been called West Virginia's "Colonial Economy," see: John Alexander Williams, *West Virginia: A Bicentennial History* (New York: W. W. Norton & Company, 1976) and Helen Matthews Lewis, et al., *Colonialism in Modern America*, (Boone, North Carolina: The Appalachian Consortium Press, 1978).

Chapter 6 Notes

1. Robert C. Brooks, *Civic Training in Switzerland: A Study of Democratic Life*, (Chicago, 1930), pp. 376–377; Agnes Bretting, "Little Germanies in the United States." Edited by Gunter Moltmann in *Germans to America 300 Years of Immigration 1683-1983*, (Stuttgart: Eugen Heinz Druck-Verlagsgesellschaft mbH), 1982, pp. 145–151.

2. Eugene Daetwyler, (Mrs.) Emil Metzener, Annie Teuscher, *The Story of Helvetia Community* (Morgantown: The Agricultural Extension Division, West Virginia University, 1923), p. 7.

3. "Der schweizerische Krankenunterstützungs-verein in Helvetia in West Virginien an seine Landsleute in der Heimat," *Handels Courier*, 15 may 1881, p. 2.,

Bern, Switzerland. (Submitted by Dr. Christian F. Stucky); John Hitz Jr., "Bericht des schweizerische Generalkonsuls über das Jahr 1875," Record Group E 2400/Washington, D.C. 1–4, pp. 309, 310.

4. David H. Sutton, Interview with Anna Merkli Mc-Neal, 22 January 1979, 26 January 1979, 25 February 1979; Interview with Eleanor Fahrner Mailloux, 30 January 1980.

5. Eugene Daetwyler, et al., *The Story of Helvetia Community*; Minutes of the Helvetia Brass Band 1921–1927. (Includes the constitutions and bylaws for the reorganization of 1898.)

6. Ibid.; Interview with Anna Merkli McNeal, 22 January 1979.

7. Ibid.

8. David H. Sutton, Interview with Margie Daetwyler, 8 January 1980; "Helvetians Win Another Battle," *Sunday Gazette Mail* (Charleston, West Virginia: May 4, 1975), p. 1C.

9. Ibid.

10. Sydney E. Ahlstrom, *A Religious History of the American People*, (New Haven and London: Yale University Press, 1972), p. 246.

11. Benjamin Holtkamp, "The German Evangelical Reformed Zions Church at Helvetia, Randolph County, West Virginia." Typewritten Manuscript, August 1, 1919. Helvetia Community Archive, Helvetia, West Virginia. NOTE: This six page synopsis was written for and submitted to the St. John's Classis of the German Reformed Church for inclusion in a history of the classis. It appeared in edited form in: Theodore Bollinger, et al., *History of St. John's Classis*, (Cleveland: Central Publishing House, 1921).

12. Ibid.; Finanzieller Bericht der Erbauung der Deutsch Evangelischer Kirche zu Helvetia, W. Va., April 1880. NOTE: This is larger than the sanctuary as it was finally built. It measures the same width, but is only 37 feet long and 13.5 feet high inside.

13. Franz Münzner, "Resolutions of the Pastor," Records of the German Evangelical Church at Helvetia, October 2, 1880; Finanzieller Bericht der Erbauung der Deutsch Kirche zu Helvetia, W. Va., April 1880, Helvetia Community Archive, Helvetia, West Virginia.

14. Benjamin Holtkamp, "The German Evangelical Reformed Zions Church."

15. Ibid., Membership Register of the German Evangelical Reformed Church, Book I, pp. 68–71, 101.

16. Minutes of the Consistory, The German Evangelical Reformed Church, 1873–1938. Helvetia Community Archive; David H. Sutton, Interviews with Anna Merkli McNeal, 24 January 1979; Ella Betler, 26 April 1979; Minnie Betler Malcomb, 6 November 1979.

17. Ibid.; Eugene Daetwyler, 18 February 1979, Tape #2.

18. David H. Sutton, Interview with Ella Betler, 26 April 1979; Interview with Anna Zumbach Daetwyler, 9 November 1979.

19. Ibid.; Interview with Genevieve Hofer, 27 November 1979.

20. Reverend Melvin E. Beck, Southeast Ohio Synod to Miss. Virginia Malcomb, 21 March 1945; Reverend Lloyd Courtney to the Consistory and Congregation, 23 September 1946. Helvetia Community Archive.

21. Robert K. Robinson to Herman Schneider, 2 April 1945; Ibid., Rev. Lloyd Courtney to the Consistory and Congregation; Draft of a letter from the Helvetia Church to the Southeast Ohio Synod asking for

release, no date. Church Records, Helvetia Community Archive; Mr. Waldo Berlekamp to the Presbyterian Church in the United States, 22 May 1947.

22.   David H. Sutton, Interview with Ella Betler, 26 April 1979.

Chapter 7 Notes

1.   Robert Redfield, *The Little Community*, (Chicago: University of Chicago Press, 1956).

2.   John A. Williams, *West Virginia: A Bicentennial History*, (New York: W. W. Norton & Company, 1976); Helen Matthews Lewis, et al., *Colonialism in Modern America*, (Boone, North Carolina: The Appalachian Consortium Press, 1978).

3.   Guy Metraux, "Social and Cultural Aspects of Swiss Immigration into the United States in the Nineteenth Century," (PhD Dissertation, Yale University, 1949).

4.   Ibid.

5.   Ibid.

6.   Paul Schenk, *The Colony Bernstadt in Laurel County, Kentucky at the Beginning of the Its Sixth Year.* Translation by S. A. Mory, (London, Kentucky, *The Sentinel Echo*, 1940).

7.   Walter Kollmorgen, "The German Swiss of Franklin Country, Tennessee: A Study of the Significance of Cultural Considerations in Farming Enterprises," (PhD Dissertation, Columbia University, 1940).

8.   Francis H. Jackson, "The German Swiss Settlement of Gruetli, Tennessee," (Masters Thesis, Vanderbilt University, Nashville, Tennessee, 1933).

9.   Ibid.

Appendix 1

*People of Swiss and German Birth Living in the Central Appalachians as Compared to Ohio
and the Nation 1870–1900*

State	Nationality	1870	1880	1890	1900
West Virginia					
	Swiss	325	810	610	696
	German	6,232	7,029	7,292	6,537
Kentucky					
	Swiss	1,133	1,094	1,892	1,929
	German	30,008	29,210	32,620	27,555
Tennessee					
	Swiss	802	1,023	1.027	1,004
	German	4,525	3,886	5,364	4,569
Ohio					
	Swiss	11,942	11,980	11,070	12,007
	German	182,889	192,597	235,668	204,160
Nation					
	Swiss	75, 145	88,621	104, 069	159,959
	German	1,690,410	1,966,742	2,784,894	2,669,164

The Statistics of the Population of the United States. 4 Vols. Ninth, Tenth, Eleventh, Twelfth Census of the United States, (Washington: Government Printing Office; 1872, 1883, 1891, 1901)

Appendix 2

Helvetia Population

The changing population of a tiny, rural, unincorporated community with no municipal or legal boundaries is a phenomenon that the United States Census is not likely to tell us much about. It is too small, too specific, and too undefined to receive attention at the level helpful to the historian. After seventy-two years, however, the government releases the original schedules of the population as they were written down by the census taker. These include the actual names, ages, occupations, national origins, and other information (depending on the census year) for each individual. These schedules comprise one of the best windows through which we can view Helvetia's population at ten-year intervals.

With a thorough knowledge of the community's social boundaries, its family names, ethnic makeup, and settlement patterns, the immigrant population can be easily discerned. The surrounding population, however, cannot be viewed except as an undefined group within the much larger boundaries of the magisterial district or county. Because this study is concerned with Helvetia primarily as an ethnic settlement, and because of the nature of the available information, the statistics concentrate on the immigrant population between the years 1869 and 1910.

The census data is only accurate, of course, to the extent that the census taker was thorough, that he understood the information given to him in often broken English, and that he was able to legibly write down what he heard. Although he can be found lacking in all of these categories, taken as a whole, the data gives a reasonably accurate picture when compared with other sources from inside the community.

By 1910, the number of people of West Virginia birth living in Helvetia had increased so much compared to those of foreign birth that the community began to blend into the local population as viewed by place of birth on the census schedule. Family names and settlement patterns then became the primary indicators, which, although useful, increased the chances of error in counting the population.

Due to the changing composition of the community after 1910, it becomes appropriate to view it more broadly than as an ethnic settlement, but the changing size and nature of the community is very difficult to document beyond this date. The ensuing timber boom certainly increased the non-Swiss and German population a great deal, but oral accounts also speak of a significant out-migration from the community during the early part of the century. After these adjustments, it is probable that the population stabilized in the 1920s and '30s before a large exodus during and after the Second World War. The latter was in keeping both with national trends toward the cities and West Virginia's continued loss of population after 1940.

Immigration into Helvetia by Year

Year	1869	1870	1871	1872	1873	1874	1875
Immigration	13	6	12	53	84	133	46
Cumulative	13	19	31	84	168	301	347

Helvetia Immigrants and Their Offspring by Place of Birth

Year	Switzerland	Germany	Various U.S. States and Canada	West Virginia (Helvetia)	Total
1870	18	2	5	1	26
1873	109	63	27	9	208
1875	192	67	90	34	381*
1880	145	48	66	85	344†
1900	93	47	60	292	492‡
1910	90	32	49	274	445

Sources: Dr. C. F. Stucky for years 1873 and 1875. U.S. Census Schedules for the years 1870, 1880, 1900, 1910

---

* The total of this column is actually 383, but Stucky gives it here and elsewhere as 381. It is unclear where he made the mistake.

† The total population as reflected in the census is 358. The total of 344 reflects the fact that in fourteen additional cases the place of birth is not given or is not readable.

‡ Figures after 1880 include West Virginia natives who married spouses of Swiss or German descent, and grandchildren of Helvetia immigrants.

Appendix 4

Life Expectancy at Various Ages for Helvetia Immigrants of Swiss and German Birth (Born between 1803–1869)

White Males	20	30	40	50	60	70	80
U.S. 1850	40.10	34.00	27.90	21.60	15.60	10.20	5.90
Helvetia	45.86	37.55	31.59	23.91	16.47	9.50	5.84
U.S. 1890	40.60	34.05	27.37	20.72	14.73	9.35	5.50
White Females	20	30	40	50	60	70	80
U.S. 1850	40.20	35.40	29.80	23.50	17.00	11.30	6.40
Helvetia	46.13	36.13	31.33	22.09	14.01	9.40	4.50
U.S. 1890	42.03	35.36	28.76	22.09	15.70	10.15	5.75

Sources: Statistical Bureau of Metropolitan Life Insurance Company; Division of Vital Statistics, National Center for Health Statistics; Bureau of the Census

Explanation of the Study

The above table shows the expectation of life at specified ages for Helvetia immigrants as compared to the general U.S. population in 1850 and 1890. The expectation of life at a specified age is the average number of years that members of a hypothetical cohort would continue to live if they were subject through the remainder of their lives to the mortality rates for specified age groups observed in a given time period.

The Helvetia study was comprised of 100 lives whose vital statistics were gathered from birth, death, and migration records of the Helvetia Reformed Church, Helvetia cemetery, family burial plots, and from U.S. census records. The immigrants were all born in either Switzerland or Germany between 1803 and 1868 and entered the community at varying ages. The data was gathered from the existing records for as many immigrants as possible, and it is therefore impossible to say whether or not the sample is exactly representative. We can account for two types of selection.

First, we were only able to gather data on people who died in the community, thus not accounting for those who moved away. To the extent which this occurred, it will tend to understate the life expectancy of the sample. In other words, it is possible, even likely, that the immigrants were even healthier than the calculations indicate.

Second, the sample is heavily weighted toward church members or at least churchgoers. Whether or not churchgoers live longer than those who do not attend church is impossible to say, but in this case, church membership greatly increased the chances of a person's vital records surviving.

To make the comparison, the sample was divided by gender and each member's year of birth, age of entry into the community, and age at death was entered into the database. The results were compared to statistics for the U.S. population in the 19th century.

Despite the limitations of the sample, there are several factors that lead to the conclusion that Helvetia immigrants were in excellent health relative to the general population and that their new environment contributed to good health for the remainder of their lives. Foremost is the fact that this study supports the observations of Dr. C. F. Stucky, who worked among the immigrant and native populations and took a special interest in all health-related matters. Stucky was a graduate of the University of Bern Medical School and had practiced for over twenty years in Switzerland and the United States before moving to Helvetia, West Virginia.

As noted, it is also likely that this study understates the life expectancy of the sample, and conversely, it is likely that the U.S. population figures are overstated because in the 19th century they were drawn from long-settled and established areas (such as Massachusetts), where health care and conditions were far better than in frontier areas. The combinations of these two biases in data would lead to a much healthier Helvetia population than the figures now indicate.

Finally, as a yardstick, the sample parallels rather evenly the life expectancies of the U.S. population, indicating that the results contain no unusual or unexpected variations.

Appendix 5

The following list of foreign-born immigrants who moved to Helvetia was compiled by cross-referencing census lists with community records. These sources can not be considered complete since the census taker sometimes missed people, and families could easily arrive and move away between the long ten-year census intervals. Church registers were also subject to omission, either due to non-membership or incomplete record keeping. Thus, the following list, while representing most of Helvetia's foreign-born population may also be incomplete. It represents a substantial compilation of materials however, which may be added to when new sources of information are brought to light.

Where possible, the country of birth and date of immigration for each person has been listed. Where this was not available, the space contains a broken line (-----). Sometimes the date given in a particular source is difficult to read or conflicts with that of other sources. A date in parenthesis, i.e., (1873), indicates the date may be incorrect due to legibility. Where sources conflict, the second date is given in parenthesis beside the first, i.e., 1873 (78). The following sources were used to compile the list:

- United States Census Schedules 1870–1910
- Helvetia graveyard and burial plot stones
- Naturalization records
- Records of the Helvetia German Reformed Church, including family registers, birth registers, death registers, membership lists, minutes of meetings

List of Foreign-Born Immigrants Who Moved to Helvetia

Name	Country of Birth	Date of Immigration	Name	Country of Birth	Date of Immigration
Ablemann, Minna	Germany	1887	Betler, Anna Mary	Switzerland	1894
Aegerter, Gottfried	Switzerland	1885	Betler, Gottlieb	Switzerland	1871
Aegerter, Marianna	Switzerland	1885	Betler, Ida	Switzerland	1873
Amlung, Albertine	Germany	1884	Betler, Verena	Switzerland	----
Amlung, George	Germany	1873	Betz, Amelia	Germany	1875
Anderegg, Amelia Lehmann	Germany	1873	Betz, George	Germany	1869
Anderegg, Eliza	Switzerland	----	Bieri, Anna	Germany	1866
Anderegg, Elizabeth	Switzerland	1874	Bieri, Ulrich	Switzerland	1879
Anderegg, George Sr.	Switzerland	1870	Birgham, Christina	Germany	1874
Anderegg, Jacob	Switzerland	1874	Birgham, Dorothea	Germany	----
Anderegg, John	Switzerland	1869	Birgham, Emma	Germany	----
Anderegg, John	Switzerland	1908	Birgham, Henry	Germany	1874
Anderegg, Mary Buehler	Switzerland	----	Birgham, Ida	Germany	1874
Asper, Henry Sr.	Switzerland	----	Birgham, William	Germany	1866
Asper, Margarette	Germany	1862	Birgham, William	Germany	----
Ast, Anna	-------	----	Blatti, Andreas	-------	----
Ast, Johannes	-------	----	Blatti, Susanna	-------	----
Bachmann, Henry	Germany	1883	Blum, Richard	Germany	----
Balli, Christian	Switzerland	1870	Bohne, Christian	Switzerland	----
Balli, Fred	Switzerland	(1870)	Bohne, Ida	Switzerland	----
Balli, John	Switzerland	(1870)	Bohne, Minna	Germany	----
Balli, Mary	Switzerland	1870	Bohne, Rebecca	Switzerland	----
Balsinger, Anna	Switzerland	(1870)	Bornhauser, Albert	Switzerland	1883
Balsinger, Elizabeth	Switzerland	1870	Bornhauser, Emma	Switzerland	1883
Balsinger, Mary	Switzerland	1870	Bornhauser, Ida	Switzerland	1883

Name	Country of Birth	Date of Immigration	Name	Country of Birth	Date of Immigration
Bornhauser, John	Switzerland	1883	Eckhardt, Henry	Germany	1862
Bornhauser, Mary	Switzerland	1883	Eckhardt, Mary	Germany	1860
Buff, John Jacob	Switzerland	1884	Eckhardt, William	Germany	1858
Buff, John	Switzerland	1882	Eggenberg, Barbara	Switzerland	----
Buff, Minna	-------	----	Eggenberg, Jakob	Switzerland	----
Bürki, Anna	Switzerland	----	Egleson, Margarette	Switzerland	1857
Bürki, Christian	Switzerland	1869	Egleson, Noah	-------	----
Bürki, Elise Dubach	Switzerland	1886	Eisenegger, Rosia	Switzerland	1867
Bürki, Elizabeth	Switzerland	----	Eisenegger, Yost	Switzerland	----
Bürki, Friedrich	Switzerland	1869	Engler, Catherine	Switzerland	1883
Bürki, Gottfried	Switzerland	1869	Engler, Christian	Switzerland	1884
Bürki, Mary	Switzerland	1869	Fahrion, Clara S.	Germany	1854
Bürki, Verena	Switzerland	1869	Fahrion, Lewis Sr.	Germany	1853
Clementz, Heinrich	-------	----	Fahrner, Gottlieb	Switzerland	1857
Clementz, Anna	-------	----	Fahrner, Katherina C.	Germany	1854
Daetwyler, Emma	Switzerland	(1874)	Favri, Elizabeth	Switzerland	----
Daetwyler, Gottlieb Sr.	Switzerland	1874	Favri, Jakob	Switzerland	----
Daetwyler, Gottlieb Jr.	Switzerland	(1874)	Fischer, Charles	Germany	1875
Daetwyler, Lena	Switzerland	1866	Fischer, Rosa	Germany	1870
Daetwyler, Magdelena	Switzerland	(1874)	Fuhrer, Anna	-------	----
Daetwyler, Paulina	Switzerland	(1874)	Fuhrer, Nicolaus	-------	----
Dubach, Elizabeth	Switzerland	1886	Gimmel, Anna	Switzerland	1872
Dubach, Frieda	Switzerland	1885	Gimmel, Catherine	Switzerland	----
Dubach, Karl	Switzerland	----	Gimmel, Christian	Switzerland	1873
Dubach, Mary	Switzerland	1885	Gimmel, Fredrick	Switzerland	1867
Dubach, Rosia	Switzerland	1885	Gobeli, Charles	Switzerland	----
Eckhardt, Barbara	Switzerland	1869	Gobeli, Fredrick	Switzerland	----

Name	Country of Birth	Date of Immigration	Name	Country of Birth	Date of Immigration
Gobeli, Jakob Sr.	Switzerland	----	Hässig, Ernest	Switzerland	1894
Gobeli, Jakob Jr.	Switzerland	----	Hässig, Rosa M.	Switzerland	1894
Gobeli, Madalina	Switzerland	----	Heller, Adolph	Switzerland	1891
Gobeli, William	Switzerland	----	Heller, Amelia	Switzerland	1891
Granville, Barbara	Switzerland	----	Heller, Anna	Switzerland	1891
Gross, Christian	-------	----	Heller, Bartholmaus	Switzerland	----
Gross, Gottlieb E.	-------	----	Heller, Frieda	Switzerland	1891
Gruber, Max	Germany	1887	Herezog, Anna	Germany	----
Güdel, Alfred	Switzerland	----	Herezog, Christopher	Germany	----
Güdel, Fredrick	Switzerland	1867	Herezog, Gustav	Germany	----
Güdel, Mary	Switzerland	1881	Hofer, Catherine (1)	Switzerland	1871
Haldemann, Elizabeth	Switzerland	1873	Hofer, Catherine (2)	Switzerland	1871
Haldemann, Fredrich	Switzerland	1872	Hofer, John Sr.	Switzerland	1871
Haldemann, John	Switzerland	1873	Hofer, John Jr.	Switzerland	1871
Haldemann, Rosanna	Switzerland	1873	Huber, Barbara	-------	----
Halder, Barbara	Switzerland	----	Huber, Casper	Switzerland	----
Halder, Jakob Sr.	Switzerland	----	Huber, Frank	Switzerland	1872
Hamilton, Barbara H.	Switzerland	1875	Huber, Fredricka	-------	----
Hartmann, Eliza	Switzerland	----	Huber, Johanna Henriette	-------	----
Hartmann, John U.	Switzerland	1866	Huber, Hulda	Switzerland	1866
Hartmann, John W.	Switzerland	1867	Huppertz, Pauline	Switzerland	1874
Hartmann, Sara	-------	----	Isch, Fredrick	-------	----
Haslebacher, Anna	Switzerland	1859	Isch, Nancy	-------	----
Haslebacher, Christina	-------	----	Isch, Rosina	Switzerland	1871
Haslebacher, Friedrich	Switzerland	1866	Isler, John B.	Switzerland	----
Haslebacher, Peter	-------	----	Jung, Fredrick	Germany	1852
Hässig, Christina	Switzerland	1894	Kaderly, Scharlotte	-------	----

Name	Country of Birth	Date of Immigration	Name	Country of Birth	Date of Immigration
Karlen, David	-------	----	Kunzler, David Jr.	Switzerland	1882
Karlen, Frederika	Germany	1860	Kunzler, Lena	Switzerland	1887
Karlen, John	Switzerland	1873	Lehmann, Adolph	Germany	----
Karlen, Katherina	Switzerland	1873	Lehmann, Christiana	Germany	1873
Karlen, Lousie	Switzerland	----	Lehmann, Clara	Germany	1882
Karlen, Paulina	Switzerland	1873	Lehmann, Helene Emilie	Germany	(1874)
Kasteler, Anna Barbara	Switzerland	----	Lehmann, Henry W.	Germany	1873
Kasteler, Christian	Switzerland	----	Lehmann, Max	Germany	1871 (76)
Kellenberger, Eliza	Switzerland	----	Lehmann, Otto	Germany	----
Kellenberger, John	Switzerland	----	Lesser, Roseli	Switzerland	----
Kern, Andrew	Switzerland	----	Lesser, Rudolph	Switzerland	----
Kern, Verena	-------	----	Lesser, Rudolph Jr.	Switzerland	----
Klee, Jakob	Switzerland	----	Leuenberger, Elizabeth	Switzerland	----
Koerner, Alfred	Germany	----	Leuenberger, John	Switzerland	----
Koerner, Caroline	Germany	1881	Looser, Anna Catherina	Switzerland	1881
Koerner, Emil	Germany	1881	Looser, Babetta	Switzerland	----
Koerner, Hermann	Germany	1881	Looser, Catherine	Switzerland	1881
Koerner, Margarett	Germany	1923	Looser, Emma	Switzerland	----
Koerner, Martha H.	Germany	1881	Looser, Frieda	Switzerland	----
Koerner, Paul	Germany	----	Looser, George J.	Switzerland	1880
Koprio, Conrad	Switzerland	1880	Looser, Ida	Switzerland	1886 (85)
Koprio, Frieda	Switzerland	----	Looser, John	Switzerland	1883
Koprio, John	Switzerland	1875 (72)	Looser, John J.	Switzerland	1880 (81)
Koprio, (Rikey)	Germany	----	Luikart, Johannes	-------	----
Kowtz, Fredrick	Germany	1897	Luikart, Maria	-------	----
Kummer, Ernest	Switzerland	1880	Lutz, Karl E.	Switzerland	(1848)
Kunzler, David Sr.	Switzerland	1882	Marti, D. (female)	Switzerland	----

Name	Country of Birth	Date of Immigration	Name	Country of Birth	Date of Immigration
Marti, Elizabeth	Switzerland	----	Moosman, Barbara	-------	----
Marti, Magdalena	Switzerland	1878	Moosman, John	-------	----
Marti, Mathias	Switzerland	1853	Müller, Anna Mary	Switzerland	1865
Marti, Rosanna	Switzerland	----	Müller, Elizabeth	Switzerland	1865
Mathey, Alfred	Switzerland	----	Müller, Ulrich	Switzerland	1865
Mathey, Arnold	Switzerland	----	Müller, Valentine	-------	----
Mathey, Arthur	Switzerland	----	Münzner, Clara	Germany	----
Mathey, Charles	-------	----	Münzner, Franz	Germany	----
Mathey, Clara	Switzerland	----	Münzner, Minna	Germany	----
Mathey, Hans	Switzerland	----	Nachtigall, Bertha	-------	1871
Mathey, Max	Switzerland	----	Nachtigall, John U.	Switzerland	1871
Mathey, Minna	Switzerland	----	Oschmann, Minna	Germany	1867
Mathey, Otto	Switzerland	----	Oschmann, Wolfgang	Germany	----
Mathey, Rosa	Switzerland	----	Pauli, Christian	Switzerland	1874
Mathey, Walter	Switzerland	----	Pauli, Edward	Switzerland	1874
McLean, Magdalina Mrs.	Switzerland	1874	Pauli, Elizabeth	Switzerland	1874
Meili, Ida	Germany	----	Pauli, Emmanuel	Switzerland	1874
Meili, Leonard	-------	----	Pauli, Ernest	Switzerland	1874
Merkli, Balthasar	Switzerland	1870	Pauli, Mary	Switzerland	1874
Merkli, Franziska	Switzerland	1870	Pauli, Theresa	Switzerland	1874
Metzener, Adolph	Switzerland	(1882)	Pensinger, Jakob	Switzerland	----
Metzener, Anna	Switzerland	1882	Pfeiffer, Rosina	Switzerland	----
Metzener, Casper	Switzerland	1882	Pickens, Pamela Mrs.	Germany	1870
Metzener, Eliza	Switzerland	1869	Prisi, Christian	Switzerland	----
Metzener, Emil	Switzerland	(1880)	Ranzinger, Barbara	Austria	----
Metzener, Margarette	Switzerland	1869	Reinhard, Benedict	-------	----
Meyer, John	Germany	----	Reinhard, Maria	-------	----

Name	Country of Birth	Date of Immigration	Name	Country of Birth	Date of Immigration
Repschlagen, Charles	Switzerland	----	Schneider, Margarett	Switzerland	1956
Repschlagen, Charlotti	Switzerland	----	Schneider, Mary	-------	----
Rexroad, Frieda Mrs.	Germany	1882	Schneider, Paul	Switzerland	----
Rohner, Elizabeth	Switzerland	1884	Schoepfle, Christian H.	Germany	----
Rohner, John (Jakob)	Switzerland	(1884)	Schroth, Daniel F.	Germany	1854
Rohner, Katherine	Switzerland	1884	Schwingel, Johannes A.	Germany	----
Roth, Christian	Switzerland	1861	Schwingel, Louise	Germany	----
Roth, Rosina	Switzerland	1851	Sennhauser, Gustav	Switzerland	1846
Rothenbuhler, Albert	Switzerland	1883	Sennhauser, Margarett	Switzerland	----
Rothenbuhler, John	Switzerland	1874	Spahr, Gottlieb	-------	----
Rufener, Christian	Switzerland	----	Spies, Henry	Germany	1886
Sacks, Erhart	Germany	----	Spies, Lena	Germany	1885
Sasse, Johannes	Switzerland	----	Sporri, Magdalena	-------	----
Sasse, Luise	-------	----	Sporri, Rudolph	-------	----
Schaefer, August	-------	----	Stadler, Barbara	Switzerland	1873
Schaefer, Margaretha L.	-------	----	Stadler, Frieda	Switzerland	1885
Schleuniger, Adela	Switzerland	1891	Stadler, George Sr.	Switzerland	1873
Schleuniger, Bertha A.	Switzerland	1891	Stadler, Katherina	Switzerland	----
Schleuniger, Ernest	Switzerland	1891	Stadler, Margarette B.	Germany	1854
Schleuniger, Martha	Switzerland	1891	Stadler, Maximillian	Germany	1849
Schleuniger, Oscar	Switzerland	1891	Steiger, Hedwig	Switzerland	1956
Schilling, Christof	------	----	Stucky, Christian F.	Switzerland	----
Schloo, Hermann	Germany	----	Stucky, Elisa	-------	----
Schnabel, C. W.	-------	----	Stucky, Gustav	Switzerland	----
Schneider, Babette	Czech Republic	(1900)	Stutzmann, John	Switzerland	1871
Schneider, Hanz	Germany	----	Stutzmann, Margarette	Switzerland	1868
Schneider, Herman	Switzerland	1906	Susli, Mathias	Switzerland	1874

Name	Country of Birth	Date of Immigration	Name	Country of Birth	Date of Immigration
Swint, Caroline	Germany	1872	Wänger, Elizabeth	-------	----
Swint, Peter	Holland (France)	1868	Wänger, Luisa	-------	----
(S), John F.	Germany	----	Wänger, Magdalina	-------	----
Teuscher, Anna (1)	Switzerland	1871	Wasmer, Elizabeth	Germany	1872
Teuscher, Anna (2)	Switzerland	1871	Wasmer, Meinrod	Germany	1872
Teuscher, John Sr.	Switzerland	1871	Wasmer, (Taraca)	Germany	(1872)
Teuscher, John Jr.	Switzerland	1871	Wenger, Catherine	Switzerland	1881
Teuscher, Magdelena	Switzerland	1871	Wenger, John	Switzerland	1881
Torgler, Anna Maria	Switzerland	----	Winkler, Elizabeth	-------	----
Torgler, Gottlieb	-------	----	Winkler, Kasper	Germany	1872
Umbrecht, Adolph	Switzerland	1882	Winkler, Samuel	-------	----
Umbrecht, (Isengor)	Switzerland	1882	Wittenbach, Mary	Switzerland	----
Umbrecht, John J.	Switzerland	1882	(Wittwer), John A	Switzerland	----
Umbrecht, Margarette	Germany	1888	Wuchner, Louis Sr.	Germany	1872
Vogel, August	Switzerland	----	Wuchner, Minnie	(Germany)	1872
Vogel, Bernard	Germany	1875	Würzer, Anna	Switzerland	(1865)
Vogel, Elizabeth	Switzerland	----	Würzer, Bertha	Switzerland	1865
Vogel, Magdelina	Switzerland	(1838)	Würzer, Elizabeth	Switzerland	(1865)
Vogel, Mattie	Switzerland	1875	Würzer, John J. Sr.	Switzerland	1865
Wälchli, Anna	Switzerland	(1854)	Würzer, John J. Jr.	Switzerland	----
Wälchli, Fredrich	Switzerland	1854	Zehnder, John	Switzerland	1851
Wälchli, John	Switzerland	(1854)	Zielmann, Anton	Switzerland	----
Wälchli, Mary	Switzerland	1854	Zielmann, Joseph	Switzerland	----
Wampfler, Samuel	Switzerland	1882	Zimmerlin, Edward	Germany	----
Wänger, Adelia	-------	----	Zimmerlin, Mary	Germany	1872
Wänger, Carles	-------	----	Zinn, Bernard	-------	----
Wänger, Christian	-------	----	Zöffel, Fredrich	Germany	1889

Name	Country of Birth	Date of Immigration
Zöffel, Henry	Germany	1889 (83)
Zöffel, Mary (1)	Germany	1889
Zöffel, Mary (2)	Germany	1889
Zogg, Anna	Switzerland	----
Zogg, Catherine	Switzerland	----
Zogg, (Florian)	Switzerland	----
Zogg, Mathias	Switzerland	----
Zogg, ( ) female	Switzerland	----
Zumbach, Anna	Switzerland	1867
Zumbach, Christian	Switzerland	1867
Zumbach, Gottlieb	Switzerland	1867
Zumbach, Jakob	Germany	1872
Zumbach, John	Switzerland	1867
Zumbach, Mary	Switzerland	----
Zürcher, Elise	Switzerland	----
Zürcher, John J.	Switzerland	----

Bibliography

Unpublished Materials

Helvetia Community Records and Collections

Helvetia, West Virginia. Helvetia Community Archive (HCA). Minutes to the Meetings of the Helvetia Brass Band 1921–1927.

Helvetia, West Virginia. HCA. Minutes to the Meetings of the Helvetia Fair Association 1917–1952.

Helvetia, West Virginia. HCA. Minutes to the Meetings of the Helvetia Farm Men's Club, Book II 1922–1935.

Helvetia, West Virginia. HCA. Records of the Helvetia Evangelical Reformed Church. Family Registers, Book I 1873–1898; Book II 1898–ca. 1950. (Includes records of membership, birth, baptism, confirmation, death, and other vital and biographical information.)

Helvetia, West Virginia. HCA. Records of the Helvetia Evangelical Reformed Church. Financial Records 1874–1899.

Helvetia, West Virginia. HCA. Records of the Helvetia Evangelical Reformed Church. Minutes to the Meetings of the Ladies Aid Society. Book I 1919–1941; Book II 1942–1958.

Helvetia, West Virginia. HCA. "The German Evangelical Reformed Zions Church at Helvetia, Randolph Country, West Virginia," Typescript by Benjamin Holtkamp, 1 August 1919.

Helvetia, West Virginia. HCA. Werner and Alma Bürki Collection.

Helvetia, West Virginia. Records of the Helvetia German Reformed Church. Minutes of the Consistory 1873–1938.

Helvetia, West Virginia. Private Collection of Genevieve Hofer. Advertising flyer written by Charles E. Lutz entitled "Helvetia Randolph County, West Virginien."

Helvetia, West Virginia. Private Collection of Genevieve Hofer. Gottlieb Hofer Photo Collection.

Helvetia, West Virginia. Private Collections. Gottfried and Walter Aegerter Photo Archives. (Selected photos are also available at the West Virginia and Regional History Collection, Morgantown, West Virginia and the West Virginia State Archive, Charleston, West Virginia.)

Unpublished Materials

Oral Interviews by David H. Sutton

The following are transcribed in full and are available both at the Helvetia Community Archive and the West Virginia and Regional History Collection, Morgantown, West Virginia.

Betler, Ella. Helvetia, West Virginia. Interviews, 16 April 1979; 25 September 1979.

Daetwyler, Anna Zumbach. Montrose, West Virginia. Interviews, 9 November 1979; 12 November 1979.

Daetwyler, Eugene. Marlinton, West Virginia. Interview, 18 February 1979.

Daetwyler, Margie Fahrner. Helvetia, West Virginia. Interview, 8 January 1980.

Fisher, Anna Sutton. Morgantown, West Virginia. Interview, 27 November 1979.

Hofer, Genevieve. Dailey, West Virginia. Interview, 10 March 1979.

Mailloux, Eleanor Fahrner. Helvetia, West Virginia. Interview, 30 January 1980.

Malcomb, Minnie Betler. Helvetia, West Virginia. Interview, 6 November 1979.

Marti, Mary Huber. Buckhannon, West Virginia. Interviews, 13 July 1979; 27 September 1979.

McNeal, Anna Merkli. Helvetia, West Virginia. Interviews, 22 January 1979; 26 January 1979; 27 January 1979; 25 February 1979; 24 April 1979.

Morris, Mary Metzener. Helvetia, West Virginia. Interview, 18 November 1979.

Ramsey, Edwin. Helvetia, West Virginia. Interview, 7 June 1979.

Sutton, Edward A. Helvetia, West Virginia. Interview, 7 January 1980.

Sutton, Helen Schneider. Helvetia, West Virginia. Interview, 29 December 1979.

UNPUBLISHED MATERIALS

American Archival and Government Repositories

Elkins, West Virginia. Randolph County Courthouse. Deed Books of Grantors and Grantees for lands in and around Helvetia.

Morgantown, West Virginia. West Virginia and Regional History Collection (WRHC). David Goff Collection.

Morgantown, West Virginia. WRHC. Gidean D. Camden Collection.

Morgantown, West Virginia. WRHC. Jonathan M. Bennett Collection.

Morgantown, West Virginia. WRHC. John S. Hoffman Collection.

Morgantown, West Virginia. WRHC. Letters of Joseph H. Diss Debar.

Morgantown, West Virginia. WRHC. Maxwell Family Papers.

Washington, D.C., The National Archives. Ninth Census of the United States: 1870. Union Township, Randolph County, West Virginia;

Tenth Census: 1880
Twelfth Census: 1900
Thirteenth Census: 1910

UNPUBLISHED MATERIALS

Swiss Archives and Government Repositories

Aarau, Switzerland. Staatsarchiv des Kantons Aargau. Bürger Register der Stadt Lenzburg.

Aarau, Switzerland. Staatsarchiv des Kantons Aargau. Bürger Register der Gemeinde Wettingen.

Bern, Switzerland. Schweizerisches Bundesarchiv. AF, E 2400/Washington, D.C. 104. John Hitz Jr., "Bericht des schweizerischen Generalkonsuls über das Jahr 1875."

Bern, Switzerland. Schweizerisches Bundesarchiv. Schweizer Gesandtschaft in Washington – Einwanderungs gesetze bis 1895. "Deutsche Colonie Helvetia, West Virginia," March 1878.

Bern, Switzerland. Schweizerisches Bundesarchiv. Schweizer Gesandtschaft in Washington – Einwanderungs gesetze bis 1895. IV Virginie Occidental. R. Lauterburg, "Das Loup Creek Unternehmen," Printed in Bern, 1880; E. Ludwig, "West Virginien Geographische Gesellschaft in Bern," *Erste Jahres Bericht 1878–1879*, G. Reymond le Brun, "Loup Creek Geographische Gesellshaft in Bern," *Zweite Jahres Bericht, 1880*.

Bern, Switzerland. Staatsarchiv des Kantons Bern. Geldstags Protokoll Vermögen und Schulden des Karl Emanuel Lutz von Bern-Hochbau Inspektor.

Bern, Switzerland. Staatsarchiv des Kantons Bern. Kontrolle über die Wohnungen der Studierenden 1834–1850.

Bern, Switzerland. Staatsarchiv des Kantons Bern. Manual des Baudepartments. Band XVIII, 24. Februar bis 19 September 1840; Band XV, 19 November 1838 bis 29 Marz 1839; Band XVI, 5 April bis 4 September 1839.

Bern, Switzerland. Staatsarchiv des Kantons Bern. Manual des Obergerichts der Republik Bern über Kriminal and Polizei Sentenzen, Band 40, 1839–1840.

Bern, Switzerland. Staatsarchiv des Kantons bern. Polizei Abteilung: Schriftenwesen – Paesse No. 3, 1847–1852.

Theses and Dissertations

Bettis, Norman C. "The Swiss Community of Highland, Illinois: A Study of Historical Geography." Masters Thesis, Western Illinois University, 1968.

Jackson, Francis H. "The German Swiss Settlement at Gruetli, Tennessee." Masters Thesis, Vanderbilt University, 1933.

Kollmorgan, Walter M. "The German Swiss in Franklin County, Tennessee: A Study of the Significance of Cultural Considerations in Farming Enterprises." PhD Dissertation, Columbia University. Washington, D.C.: Department of Agriculture, 1940.

Metraux, Guy S. "Social and Cultural Aspects of Swiss Immigration into the United States in the 19th Century." PhD Dissertation, Yale University, 1949.

Partadiredja, Atje. "Helvetia, West Virginia: A Study of Pioneer Development and Community Survival in the Appalachia." PhD Dissertation, University of Wisconsin, 1966.

Smith, Edwin A. "Helvetia, The Swiss Land of West Virginia." Term Paper, West Virginia University, 1960.

Wegman, Werner. "Nationality Group in the Rural Population: A Sociological Study." Masters Thesis, West Virginia University, 1942.

Wilmoth, Troy Bell. "Swiss Communities in Randolph County." Masters Thesis, West Virginia University, 1937.

Wilson, Donald E. "Joseph H. Diss Debar in West Virginia." Masters Thesis, West Virginia University, 1961.

Published Materials.

Arlettaz Gerald. *Etudes et Sources, Emigration et colonisation suisses en Amerique 1815–1918.* Bern: Archives Federales Suisses, 1979.

Balmer, Hans Fredrich. *Die Kolonie Bernstadt, Kentucky in ihrer geschichtlichen Entwicklung und ihrem gegenwärtigen Stände: Ein Beitrag zur Geschichte der Schweizerkolonien.* Bern and New York, 1884.

Bennett, Avah. "Helvetia." *West Virginia Review,* (August 1935).

Bollinger, Rev. Theodore P. *History of St. John's Classis.* Cleveland: Central Publishing House, 1921.

Bonjour, Edgar. *A Short History of Switzerland,* Oxford: Clarendon Press, 1952.

Bosworth, Albert S. *A History of Randolph County, West Virginia.* Elkins, West Virginia: By the Author, 1916; reprinted ed. Parsons, West Virginia: McClain Printing Company, 1975.

Brooks, Maurice. "Tiny Spot of Old Switzerland Is Brought to the Mountains of West Virginia." *Parkersburg Sentinel,* 25 June 1948, p. 20.

Brunner, Otto. *Die Auswanderung nach den Vereinigten Staaten Nord-Amerikas, amerikanische landwirtschaftliche Verhältnesse und ein neues Ansiedlungsprojekt.* Bern: Kommissions-Verlag von Huber u. Cie., 1881.

Buhlmann, Walter A. *The Swiss Society of New York: Golden Jubilee 1882–1932.* New York, 1932.

Cambell, John C. *The Southern Highlander and His Homeland.* New York, 1921; reprinted Lexington, Ky., 1969.

Cometti, Elizabeth. "Swiss Immigration to West Virginia: A Case Study." *Mississippi Valley Historical Review* No. 1 (June 1960), pp. 66–87.

Cornell, F. D. *Trends in West Virginia Agriculture.* College of Agriculture, West Virginia University Bulletin 276, July 1936.

Daetwyler, Eugene C., [Mrs.] Emil Metzener, and Annie Teuscher. *The Story of Helvetia Community.* Morgantown, West Virginia; The Agricultural Extension Service, 1923.

David, Nettie Vass. "Helvetia, West Virginia's Swiss Village." *West Virginia Review.* (December 1934), p. 80.

Defour, Perret. *The Swiss Settlement of Switzerland County, Indiana.* Indianapolis: Indiana Historical Commission, 1925.

Diss Debar, Joseph H. *The West Virginia Handbook and Immigrant's Guide.* Parkersburg, West Virginia: Gibbons Bros., 1870.

Eidenbenz, Fred, ed. *North American Swiss Alliance Jubilee Book, 1865–1940.* New York, 1941.

Faust, Albert B. *A Guide to the Materials for American History in Swiss and Austrian Archives.* Washington, 1916.

Grueningen, John Paul von. *The Swiss in the United States.* Madison, Wisconsin: The Swiss American Historical Society, 1940.

------------ *Eine Kurze Beschreibung der Saaner-Kolonie nahe bei Stanford in Lincoln Country, Kentucky.* Frankfort, Kentucky, 1882.

Guggisberg, Hans R. *Alte und Neue Welt in historischer Perspektive.* Bern u. Frankfurt/M.; Verlag Herbert Lang. & Cie, 1973.

"Helvetians Win Another Battle," *Sunday Gazette Mail,* Charleston, W. Va., 4 May 1975, p. 1C.

Herold, Christopher J. *The Swiss Without Halos.* New York: Columbia University Press, 1948.

Hutchinson, Jonathan A. *Land Titles in Virginia and West Virginia.* Cincinnati: Robert Clark and Co., 1887.

Lewis, Helen Mathews, et al. *Colonialism in Modern America.* Boone, NC: The Appalachian Consortium Press, 1978.

Lorentz, Anne. "Swiss Village Thrives in West Virginia Hills." *Clarksburg Telegram,* 30 September 1930.

Kemper, Charles E., ed. "Documents Relating to a Proposed Swiss and German Colony in the Western Part of Virginia." *Virginia Magazine of History and Biography,* Vol. XXIX (April 1921), pp. 183–190; (July 1921), pp. 287–291.

Martin, William. *Switzerland from Roman Times to the Present.* New York and Washington: Praeger Press, 1971.

Mayer, Kurt. *The Population of Switzerland.* New York: Columbia University Press, 1952.

Meier, Heinz K. *The United States and Switzerland in the Nineteenth Century.* The Hague, The Netherlands: Mouton & Co., Publishers, 1963.

------------ *Friendship Under Stress: U.S.- Swiss Relations 1900-1950.* Bern: Herbert Lang & Co., 1970.

Meynen, Emil. *Bibliography on German Settlements in Colonial North America 1683-1933.* Leipzig, 1937.

Nelson, Arnold E. et al. *Haven In the Hardwood: A History of Pickens, West Virginia,* Parsons, W. Va.: McClain Printing Co., 1971.

Netting, Robert. *Balancing On An Alp: Ecological Change and Continuity in a Swiss Mountain Community.* Cambridge: Cambridge University Press, 1981.

Preysz, Clara M. "The Swiss Settlement of Alpena, West Virginia." *Randolph County Historical Society Magazine of History and Biography.* Vol. 9, 1937, pp. 33–37.

Rice, Harvey Mitchell, *The Life of Jonathan M. Bennett: A Study of the Virginias in Transition.* Chapel Hill: North Carolina University Press, 1943.

Schelbert, Leo. "On Becoming an Immigrant: A Structural View of the 18th and 19th Century Swiss Data." *Perspectives in American History.* (Cambridge, Mass. 1973), pp. 439–495.

Schelbert, Leo, ed. *New Glarus 1845–1970: The Making of the Swiss American Town.* Glarus, Switzerland: Tschudi & Cie. Kommissionsverlag, 1970.

----------- *Einführung in die schweizerishe Auswanderungsgeschichte Der Neuzeit.* Zürich: Verlag Staübli, 1976.

Schenk, Paul. *Die Kolonie Bernstadt in Laurel County, Kentucky am Beginne ihres sechsten Lebensjahres.* Frankfort, Ky., 1886. (Was translated into English by Samuel A. Mory and printed in London, Ky. in 1940 by *The Sentinel Echo*.)

"Serving West Virginia's Unique Swiss Community," *Employee Newspaper of the C&P Telephone Company of West Virginia.* (Vol. 1, No. 38) December 30, 1966.

Staehelin, Ernst, "Schweizer Theologen im Dienste der reformierten Kirche in den Vereinigten Staaten:. *Schweizerische Theologische Zeitschrift,* XXXVI (1919).

Steinach, Adelrich. *Geschichte und Leben der Schweiser Kolonien in den Vereinigten Staaten von Nord-Amerika.* New York: By the Author, 1889.

Stucky, Christian F. "Der schweizerische Krankenunterstützungsverein in Helvetia West Virginien an seine Landsleute in der Heimat." *Handels Courier,* 15 May 1881, p. 2.

Stutler, Boyd. B. "Joseph H. Diss Debar, Prophet, Colonizer," *West Virginia Review.* (December 1931), pp. 154–156.

Summers, Festus P. *Johnson Newlon Camden: A Study In Individualism.* New York, London: G. P. Putnam's Sons, 1937.

Sutton, David. H. "Ella Betler Remembers Helvetia" and "A West Virginia Swiss Community: The Aegerter Photographs of Helvetia, Randolph County." *Goldenseal,* Vol. 6, No. 2, April–June 1980.

"Swiss Visitors to West Virginia," *Wheeling Register,* 14 April 1880.

"Teuton Flag Cause of War in Helvetia," *The Weekly New Dominion,* Morgantown, W. Va., 18 April 1917.

Theiler, Miriam B. *New Glarus' First 100 Years.* Madison, Wisconsin: Campus Publishing Co., 1946.

Turney, Robert S. "The Encouragement of Immigration in West Virginia 1863–1871." *West Virginia History.* (October 1950), pp. 46–60.

Wegman, Werner. "The Helvetia Community," *Randolph County Historical Society Magazine of History and Biography.* Vol. 10, (1942), pp. 17–36.

Williams, John A. *West Virginia: A Bicentennial History.* NY: W. W. Norton & Company, 1976.

Index

About the Author

DAVID H. SUTTON is a native of Helvetia, West Virginia. He received his Bachelors Degree from Davis & Elkins College and Masters in History from West Virginia University. As an archivist and manuscripts curator, he has worked for the Washburn Norlands Foundation in Livermore Falls, Maine and the Balch Institute for Ethnic Studies in Philadelphia. He currently makes his home in New Hampshire.